# Royal Houghton

## The Story of Houghton Regis
## Bedfordshire

## Pat Lovering

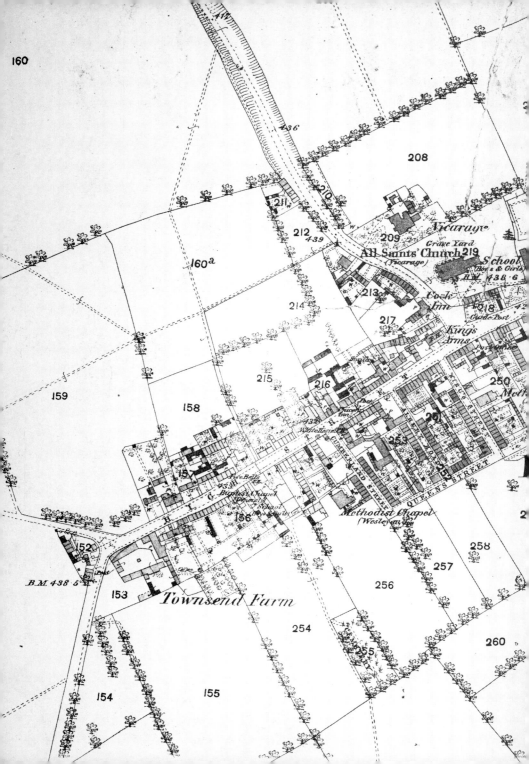

First published November 1986
by The Book Castle
12 Church Street, Dunstable

Text © Pat Lovering
Line Illustrations © Elizabeth Lowen

Printed by White Crescent Press Ltd, Luton

ISBN 0 9509773 1 4

# Royal Houghton

by

**Pat Lovering**

original research by

**Vivienne Evans**

line illustrations by

**Elizabeth Lowen**

# PREFACE

People still find parish churches a fascination, so that week by week visitors to our church for weddings and baptisms especially stop to ask questions. How old is the church? where did Regis come from? These and many other questions are the beginning of the fascinating trail taking us back nearly one thousand years. Telling the story of a single parish in just a few chapters is no easy task, especially when as in this case some of the major events in English history have left their marks. The willingness of our author in undertaking this project, with the intention not only of telling the story but ensuring the future dignity of the present town and its historic churches, are reasons for admiration and gratitude from all those who live and work here in Houghton today. Pat Lovering having also lived and worshipped regularly in Houghton Regis, has been able to produce a book of very great interest and with warmth and affection for the subject. I warmly commend this book and very much hope that the story of Houghton Regis will inspire this same loyalty, interest and affection for our heritage in the younger and the older members of our locality who may read it. Then it may have played its part in furthering the spirit of our new town in the decades ahead.

G M Neal
Vicar of
Houghton Regis

i

# ACKNOWLEDGEMENTS

When Houghton Regis Parochial Church Council asked Vivienne Evans to research the history of Houghton Regis and of All Saints Church, it little dreamed of the wealth of interesting material that she would find. Mrs Evans has had the difficult task of supplying the contents of this book; I have merely written the narrative from her notes. I must say at this point that any errors of misinterpretation or assumption are entirely mine, however, and to thank her for all her patient assistance with this project.

I would also like to thank the people who have kindly lent me their treasured photographs (they are acknowledged individually at the back of the book). I am most grateful to John Bailey for allowing me to reproduce his drawing of Calcutt Farm, to John Lunn for his advice on the Fraternity of the Holy Trinity, to Rosemary Harris, who is mentioned in the bibliography, for the generous sharing of her research into the Brandreth family, and to Elizabeth Lowen for her delightful line drawings.

My thanks too to Gloria Underwood, Emma Beardsmore, Alan Crisp and Trevor Wood who have done so much to prepare the manuscript. The P.C.C. is particularly grateful to Paul Bowes of the Book Castle who has been a most supportive publisher.

Royalties from the sale of "Royal Houghton" go towards the Restoration Appeal of All Saints Church, Houghton Regis, the oldest building now remaining in the new town; our thanks are also due to you, therefore, for buying the book and thus helping towards the restoration of a Grade 1 listed building.

Pat Lovering

## RESEARCH FUNDING

Houghton Regis Parochial Church Council provided the initial funding, but the cost of the very detailed reserach necessary for this book has been met by generous help from

Bedfordshire County Library

Robinson & White Ltd
Icknield House, 40 West Street, Dunstable

and from

Barb Carpets, 57-59 St Peters Road, Dunstable

The Book Castle, 12 Church Street, Dunstable

Dunstable Museum Trust

Rosemary Finch, B Phar M.P.S.,
118 High Street North, Dunstable

G.E.M. Office Systems Ltd.,
3 Brittany Court, High Street South, Dunstable

The Rural Community Council

The University of Cambridge Board of Extra-Mural Studies.

# CONTENTS

End-paper: Quick Reference Guide to the Interior of
           the medieval Church of All Saints.

Fig. 1  All Saints Church, Houghton Regis. (O.R.)

# CHAPTER 1

## BEGINNINGS

The whole area in which Houghton Regis lies is rich in the most ancient history. The surrounding hills have been occupied and settled from the very earliest times mainly because, as the last ice age retreated, the chalk hills of the Chilterns were left standing above very difficult terrain. Chalk drains quickly and is inhospitable to trees which like plenty of moisture, so the hill ridges were covered only in grass or light brushland making them easy to traverse, and later more easily cleared for cultivation, an important factor when only primitive farm implements were available. The land below was heavily wooded or marshy and generally difficult both to traverse and to farm.

New Stone Age man farmed in a primitive way at Puddlehill in the western part of the parish, and there are indications that this site was occupied from Neolithic times onwards.

Before Watling Street was cut through the chalk and separated them, Puddlehill and Maidenbower were on the same piece of downland. The site of Maidenbower was surrounded by a series of deep ditches and banks in Neolithic times, and populated and enlarged over a long period. It was thought to be a religious and/or defensive centre for the area. It lies by the western boundary of the parish.

With constant use, the downland migrant areas became trodden into well-worn paths, from the coast inland. One of these paths was the Icknield Way, an ancient British way running from east to west of Houghton Regis. However, areas which were easily reached by traders and settlers were equally easily reached by raiders and invaders; at times, Houghton was troubled by both. Pottery used by the aggressive Catuvellaunis (of Wheathamstead and St Albans) has been found at Northfields in the northern part of the parish, and there is some evidence that they attacked Maidenbower.

Beneath present day Dunstable lie the remains of the Roman town of Durocobrivae. This town was on the military road (Watling Street) built by the Romans from London to Wales and the north west. It crossed the Icknield Way from south to north in the centre of the town, making an important trading and staging place. Farmers from what we call Houghton would have found a ready market in the town.

Remains of a Roman temple at Houghton Regis are currently being investigated by the Manshead Archeological Society.

During its long occupation, the Roman army used their network of roads to defend the country and to prevent civil unrest. However, when the soldiers departed, around 400 AD, there was constant coastal attack and a break down of law and order. Saxon mercenaries were brought in and the countryside was peaceful until financial support for the mercenaries was withdrawn and unpaid groups of soldiers terrorised the neighbourhood making the roads unsafe and town life impossible.

Eventually, Durocobrivae was deserted.

Then according to the Anglo Saxon Chronicles, in 571 a Saxon army under a warrior called Cutha won a decisive victory over the Romano-British and swept triumphantly along the Icknield Way from Limbury to Aylesbury and beyond leaving the whole area under Saxon rule and relatively safe for Saxon immigrants to settle.

There is no record of when exactly the area around All Saints Church was settled, but the name Houghton comes from the Saxon 'hoe', the spur of a hill, and 'tun' a village. There is a strong tradition locally that the Saxon prefix 'Saelig' Houghton preceded the use of King's Houghton, or Houghton Regis. 'Saelig' means holy or fortunate and many local residents can remember 'Saelig Houghton' being rendered as "silly Houghton".

Houghton's lush meadowland and abundant water supply would have made it an attractive proposition for Saxon farmers. With the source of the River Lea nearby, the whole area has water in "fast running streams" as the old maps have it, or very near the surface. There were several large ponds in the village still at the turn of the last century.

Another point in favour of settling on the land near the present church was, of course, that it was a reasonable distance away from Watling Street and the Icknield Way which would have been hazardous even in relatively peaceful times.

At the end of the 8th Century, the Saxon way of life was disturbed by fearsome Danish raiders coming inland to rob, burn and loot. Eventually, the Danes invaded and in 878 the country was divided between Saxons and Danes.

Unfortunately, Houghton found itself in the unhappy position of being on the border between the two factions, doubtless harried by raiding parties from both sides. The Anglo Saxon Chronicles record an occasion in 913 when the Danes set out to raid Luton but the local people were so incensed by constant harrassment and attack that they resisted and not only drove off the aggressors but also captured a good part of their horses and weapons.

In the end the Saxon kings managed to drive back the Danes, gradually reducing the area that they occupied, King Aethelstan (924-939) united England and peace and stability returned.

By the time of Edward the Confessor (1042 - 1066) the shires were established. Much of South Bedfordshire had become Royal land but the exact date of this is unknown. Houghton was a Royal manor, and evidently a prosperous one, since it paid a high money tax to the King. This sort of tax was usually only paid by towns, not agricultural villages.

Houghton was the King's demesne land, that is it was for his household use, so the villagers also had to provide from their land enough wheat, honey and other things to support the Royal household for half a day. It had one of only four self-supporting churches in Bedfordshire and its area covered most of what is now Dunstable plus a part of Lewsey Farm, Luton.

Where the Roman road crossed the Icknield Way, Houghton land was on three sides of the crossroads. To the south, the boundary ran along the bottom of Blows Downs (where Jeans Way is now) as far as Watling Street. This area between Blows Downs and the Icknield Way was Houghton grazing ground. The boundary then ran along the Icknield Way on the West Street side as far as the Green Lane. The western boundary of Houghton land then followed the line of Green Lane, and included Maidenbower and Sewell. The northern side was just beyond and incorporated Thorn, Calcutt Farm and what is now Grove Farm, before the boundary formed the eastern side which included the present Parkside and the land west of Poynters Road which is now Lewsey Farm, before joining up with the southern boundary once more at Blows Downs.

Sewell was part of Houghton land, but Edith, wife of Edward the Confessor, separated Sewell from Houghton and gave it to her "man" Walraven, possibly as a pension. The Sheriff of Bedfordshire returned it to the King's manor of Houghton, and it is part of the parish now, but because of this brief separation Sewell has its own entry in the Domesday Book, and the families who subsequantly lived in the old manor house there continued to regard themselves as a separate manor.

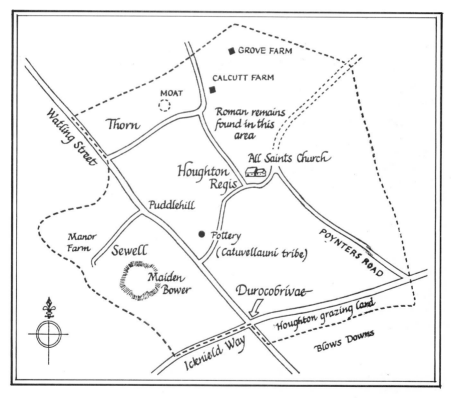

Fig. 2.    A sketchmap showing the original boundaries of Houghton Regis.

# CHAPTER 2

## THE DOMESDAY BOOK

Unfortunately, no written evidence of Saxon Houghton has survived.

After the defeat of King Harold at Hastings in 1066, William the Conqueror led his victorious army round London to Berkhamstead. The church and secular leaders invited him in to London to become the next King but the Anglo Saxon Chronicles record that "nevertheless, in the meantime they harried everywhere they came".

As was usual, the soldiers lived off the land that they passed through, but William sent officials ahead of the army to claim the demesne land of Edward the Confessor in his (William's) name, and this land was left unharmed. Houghton, Sewell, Kensworth and part of Caddington were claimed in this way and left alone, but elsewhere the ravaging army advanced, killing the plough oxen, baking seed corn, imprisoning anyone who complained, taking anything they needed and drastically impoverishing the countryside as they passed.

William I rewarded the noblemen who had come with him and helped him in his victory. He gave them land (judiciously scattered so that no one person could become too powerful and prove a threat to him) which they shared with friends and relatives. In turn, the friends and relatives put in ex-soldiers and other loyal followers as tenants. In this way, William the First's chamberlain came to "hold" (rent) scattered pieces of land in Bedfordshire, including church land in Houghton. William I now owned personally all of Houghton including the land round the crossroads.

The country became reasonably peaceful, and William I launched the Domesday survey after "very deep discussion with his council about this country" (Anglo Saxon Chronicles) at Gloucester during Christmas 1085.

The Domesday Survey was so called because men thought its findings would stand until the day of Judgement, so detailed was it. The compiler of the Anglo Saxon Chronicles unconsciously mirrors the affront of those under scrunity "So very narrowly did he have (each shire) investigated that there was no single hide not a yard of land nor indeed (shame it is to relate it but it seemed no shame to him to do) was one ox or one cow or one pig left out that was not put down in his record". The survey included a record of all land owned by the King in each shire, and what dues he ought to have annually, and was basically a sort of tax register.

The Domesday Book gives information about each village in 1086 ("the value of this land is...") and at 1066 ("and was..."). These values are the same for Houghton and Sewell, because the land was protected from the ravages of William's army in 1066, but the value of the part of Caddington, which for example was not so protected, fell from £5 per year in 1066 to ten shillings (50p) in 1086.

The entries for Houghton and Sewell are:

> M. HOUGHTON (Regis), a household manor of the King's, answers for 10 hides. Land for 24 ploughs. In lordship 2 ploughs. The villagers, 22 ploughs.

38 villagers and 12 smallholders.

Meadow for 12 ploughs; woodland, 100 pigs.
In total, it pays £10 a year by weight and
half a day (day's provisions) in wheat,
honey and other things which belong to the
king's revenue; from petty customary dues
and from 1 pack-horse 65s; from customary
dog dues 65s; to the Queen 2 ounces of gold;
from the increase which Ivo Tallboys put on
£3 by weights and 20s in white silver; 1
ounce of gold to the Sheriff.

William the Chamberlain holds the church of
this manor, with 1/2 hide which belongs to
it.  It is of the 10 hides of the manor.
Land for 1/2 plough; it is there.  Value 12s
a year.

SEWELL answered for 3 hides before 1066.
Land for 2 ploughs.  1 1/2 there; a further
1/2 possible.

Meadow for 4 oxen.
1 villager and 4 smallholders.
The value of this land is and was 20s.

   The Domesday Book, then, gives us the first written
record of a church on the present site.  No details
are given of the building since churches were not
taxed, and no priest is mentioned.

   We are told that the church was supported by 1/2
hide of land (about 60 acres); it was worth 12
shillings per year and had 4 oxen to pull a light
plough.  It was part of the Manor of Houghton and the
38 villagers and 12 smallholders who lived on the
manor would have had to share the work on the church
land.  The rector was also rector of Luton, (formerly
a wealthy Saxon priest called Morcar, but later
William the Chamberlain) and would have owned the

produce of the church land and also one-tenth of everything all the families in the village produced, made and collected.

Houghton was a sizeable village - it probably had the highest population of any village community with the same acreage in either Bedfordshire or Hertfordshire, and a higher population per acre than either of the King's market-villages of Luton or Leighton. If we consider that for every working man there were about five other members of his family - wife, children, parents - then we can multiply the 50 men by 5 to arrive at a rough estimate of the population, say 250. There were only 5 people working at Sewell, say 25 in all and we can see it was in poor shape, because although there was arable land sufficient to need 2 ploughs and 16 oxen, there were only 12 oxen there. So the combined population would be about 275 people.

Houghton was a royal village and was listed among the "royal" possessions which start the list in every county. It would appear to be a prosperous village, since unlike every other village in Bedfordshire and Hertfordshire it was in a position to find a large, money tax, such taxes usually only being collected in towns.

It may well be that nearness to a busy crossroads in time of relative peace contributed to Houghton's prosperity.

Twelve of the Houghton residents were small-holders who had some craft with which to support their families and the rest were classed as villagers, that is, agricultural labourers. Vivienne Evans in her history of Dunstable puts forward the theory that several of the Houghton "small-holders" were trading at the crossroads. She points out that the travelling clerks collecting information for the survey had no "column" for anything out of the ordinary.

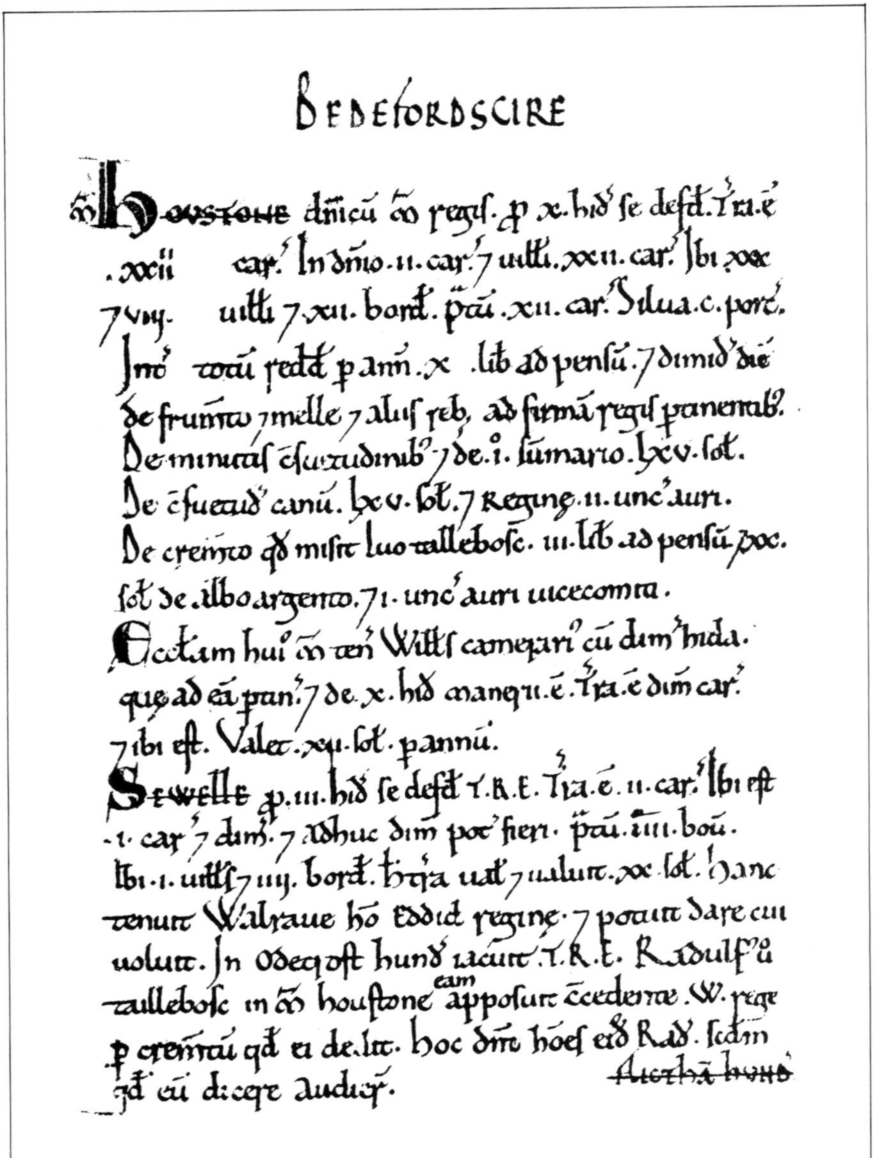

# BEDEFORDSCIRE

Houstone dnicu co regis. p. x. hid se defd. Tra e
.xxii. car. In dnio .ii. car. 7 uilli. xxii. car. Ibi xx
7 viii. uilli 7 .xii. bord. pra .xii. car. Silua .c. porc.
In tou redd p ann .x. lib ad pensu. 7 dimid die
de frumto 7 melle 7 aliis reb, ad firma regis ptinentib.
De minutis csuetudinib 7 de .i. sumario .lxv. sol.
De csuetud canu .lxv. sol. 7 Regine .ii. unc auri.
De cremto qd misit suo tallebosc .iii. lib ad pensu xx.
sol de albo argento. 7 i. unc auri uicecomra.

Eccltam hui m ten Wills camerari cu dim hida.
que ad eu ptin. 7 de .x. hid manqu e. Tra e dim car.
7 ibi est. Valet. xii. sol. pannu.

Sewelle p. iii. hid se defd T.R.E. Tra e .ii. car. Ibi est
.i. car 7 dim. 7 adhuc dim pot fieri. pra .iiii. bou.
Ibi .i. uilli 7 iiii. bord. Inta ual 7 ualut. xx sol. Hanc
tenuit Walraue ho Eddid regine. 7 potuit dare cui
uoluit. In odecqost hund iacuit T.R.E. Radulf u
tallebosc in m houstone eam apposuit ccedente .W. rege
p cremtau qd ei de.lit. hoc dnt hoes eid Rad. scdm
qd eu dicere audier. <del>Aierha hund</del>

---

Fig. 3.    The Domesday entry for the Royal Manor of
Houstone (Houghton Regis).

10

"(The small-holders) were not free burgesses
(businessmen). They were tied to the land
and landlord in the feudal way but neither
were they villagers with large amounts of
arable land with which to supports their
families, nor were they landless serfs. So
the only column under which to put them was
"small-holder" which basically they were, as
trading was probably a sideline".

The Domesday survey then, gives us an interesting
picture of a sizeable village, a royal property,
important enough to have its own church and pay a
large money tax, and benefitting from its position and
the enterprise of its residents.

# CHAPTER 3

## THE SAXON CHURCH

There is no written record of who originally built All Saints Church, or when. As we have seen, "The church of this manor" is mentioned in Domesday, with 60 acres of land to support it, but no details are given since the Domesday survey was a tax assessment and churches were not taxed. This was a royal village of some value so the church was probably a stone building.

The churches at Luton and at Houghton were linked closely together in their early history. A 19th century Rural Dean and Rector of Luton, the Reverend Cobbe, made the history of Luton Church (and consequently that of Houghton church) his lifetime's study. He makes suggestions of 8th Century Kings and dates, but this is of course speculation. Edward the Confessor, the saintly King, was responsible for church building in nearby Hertfordshire, but there is no evidence to suggest who originally built All Saints.

We can however, take up the story before the Norman conquest.

The Domesday tax survey gives us figures and information referring to the period before 1066 and then referring to 1086, the time of the actual survey.

In 1066 Morcar, a Saxon priest held

i.      the church of Luton and the five hides of
        Dollow Manor
ii.     as a private possession, he held one hide
        (about 120 acres) in Potsgrove
iii.    also as a private possession a half hide (about
        60 acres) in Battlesden.

In addition

iv.     Houghton, adjoining Luton on the King's land,
        had a church with half a hide (60 acres) to
        support it.   No priest is mentioned, but
        undoubtedly Morcar was also in charge of this
        church.

The King's land in Luton and Houghton was undamaged
in 1066 and its value remained the same in 1086, but
the value of Morcar's privately owned land dropped
dramatically after William's army had passed through.

Morcar must have been an important person, since a
church living of five hides was a valuable gift,
especially on Royal land.

We do not know what happended to Morcar.   He may
have died conveniently and left the livings vacant,
but in other cases where this happened (as at Leighton
Buzzard Church, for example) another priest was
appointed.

William, the next holder of the land, is described
as the King's Chamberlain.   This was a secular post,
an administrative position of the kind we would
associate with the Senior Civil Service.   At the time
of the Domesday survey, in 1086 he 'held' (rented), in
Bedfordshire

i.   the lands of Luton church
ii.  the land of Houghton church

iii. the one hide at Potsgrove
and iv. the half hide at Battlesden 'which were
     formerly owned by Morcar the priest.'
v.   in Buckinghamshire he held two hides at Hartswell
(near Aylesbury)

He joined all this land together as one 'manor'
which proved highly inconvenient for the men at
Hartswell. In the 15th Century they are always
receiving a standard fine for not attending the Manor
Court at Dollow (Luton)!

Like most court clerks, William the Chamberlain
would probably have received his education in a
monastery, but there is no evidence that he was a
clergyman. He was certainly given much church land,
but never acted as a priest and made all his church
land into secular land. We assume that he was
married, since he had a son.

He received his church lands at Luton and Houghton
as a reward for leaving Normandy and chancing his
fortunes with William I, and he did not want to risk
losing them to a clergyman. So to make the land not
only legally his, but also in a form he could bequeath
to his son, he made the entire new manor into a
'half-knights' fee, in other words, he changed it from
free alms (free from a military valuation) into the
same type of assessment as most other land - a
military fief. This meant that from then on, the
holders of these lands had to provide half the cost of
keeping an armed soldier at war for forty days in
every year.

The effect of this on both Houghton and Luton was
that they were left with churches, but no financial
means of supporting a priest. Even the tithes went to
William the Chamberlain.

We can only speculate as to what happened - no doubt
visiting priests came to the churches from time to

time, and William may have paid for a part-trained
deacon.    There are no details of how the churches
managed during the reigns of William I and II.

When William II inherited this country, he had very
little interest in it; his one aim was to raise as
much money as possible. All land or jobs went to the
highest bidder. When a priest or even a bishop died,
he left the position vacant for years at a time, so
that he could take the revenues from it for his own
use.   He was not likely to interfere if one of his
officials held land intended for the church.

William the Chamberlain died.   His son William II
was Chamberlain to the King as his father had been.

Henry I came to the throne in 1100.   A terrible
disaster overtook him in 1120 when he was returning
from Normandy. One of his boats was lost. His two
sons, a daughter and many of their friends were
drowned.

As a result, the next year Henry I strengthened the
position of his illegitimate son Robert.   He created
an earldom for him, giving him much land including the
manor of Dollow (Luton).   Robert, Earl of Gloucester,
was a sincere Christian and supported the Church.

Both William Chamberlain 2 and Earl Robert were
often at King Henry's court at home and overseas.   At
times they were both witness to the same royal deeds.
On these occasions, William would sign 'William of
Hocton' (Houghton), and since he did not hold the
village of Houghton, but only the church land, this
gives some idea of the value he put upon this part of
his inheritance.

The old church at Luton was still standing, but Earl
Robert ordered a new one to be built, not on the
King's land, but on land of his own, under or near the
present parish church.   It is recorded that he took

down the Saxon church until 'not one stone stood upon another'. The most obvious reason for building a new church on his own land was to get the 'advowson' (the right to appoint a priest). This new church was probably built between 1121 and 1131, since at the end of his reign King Henry was abroad and Earl Robert was with him.

When Henry died in 1135 once again distant events had their repercussions in the village. The rightful heiress to the throne was Earl Robert's step-sister Matilda, but Henry's nephew Stephen was crowned King and Matilda was ignored. Earl Robert stayed abroad for twelve months, but in the end he acknowledged King Stephen and returned home.

King Stephen was grateful for the support of the highly-respected Earl of Gloucester, and he not only confirmed his right to all his lands, he added the advowson of Luton Church to the Earl's property. Houghton is not mentioned by name, but the Earl also received that advowson (date unkown) so the two were probably linked by custom.

Earl Robert wanted to give the living to Gilbert de Cymmay, who is thought to have been a young relative or a friend. King Stephen agreed and together they presented Gilbert to the Bishop of Lincoln as their choice. Powerful patronage, one would have thought.

However, William Chamberlain 2 was also a person of some influence. Although the Bishop agreed that it was wrong for William to hold church lands he hesitated to actually turn him out. His solution sounds strangely familiar to us — he set up a committee of enquiry!

William refused to attend. He wrote and told the Bishop that he had not received the land as a church living, but had inherited it as a military fief. The representative of the parishioners then wrote to the Bishop and asked the Bishop outright if the land in question really belonged to the Church. If so, it should be restored with the church to its ecclesiastical rights.

The Bishop arranged for the committee to meet in Luton, and King Stephen issued a writ requiring the people of Luton to give evidence. Once again, Houghton is not mentioned by name, but we can take it that Houghton representatives were there as interested parties.

The men of Luton stated categorically that the five hides of land were originally given in free alms and remained so until 'the last William' who turned the liberties of the church into a military fief.

It was obvious that the land was not really the property of the first William to pass on to his son. The Bishop felt safe enough to take over the income from the church and church lands, but still not safe enough to appoint Gilbert de Cymmay!

However, by now Earl Robert was no longer a friend of King Stephen. He had gone to join his step-sister Matilda, and when he returned it was as King Stephen's enemy! There was a short civil war during which Earl Robert proved to be on the losing side. He was captured and lost all his estates in England, but King Stephen allowed Gilbert de Cymmay to 'own' (organise) the church in Luton.

When Henry II came to the throne in 1154, Earl Robert was dead. His heir was Earl William of Gloucester.

Earl William had given a 'fee' (a parcel of lands) to St Albans abbey in 1153, and this fee contained both Houghton and Luton churches and 'the land which William the Chamberlain held.' The gift is recorded in official documents because it involved royal land and, at a later date, it appears in a list of gifts compiled at the Abbey.

It appears that Henry II in his turn, seized the church lands, but quickly relinquished them presumably to the Abbey. Henry "confirmed" his father's possessions to Earl William and they agreed that Gilbert should remain as what would now be called rector of the church.

The name Houghton does not appear in all these legal papers, but at every stage the pattern of events for All Saints Church is exactly the same as that for Luton.

Despite some further dispute, Houghton Church and its land was owned by St Albans Abbey from 1153 to the dissolution. The profits were to be used for hospitality to pilgrims.

Houghton had a vicarage created and endowed well in advance of most South Beds villages. The original endowment seems to be lost but reference to it appears in the book of endowments in the Diocese of Lincoln at the time of Bishop Hugh of Wells (1209 - 1235). In 1226 the living was vacant and Stephen de Heredwike was presented by the Abbey. The value of the endowment was given as" a hundred shillings or more". This was made up of altar offerings and the "small" tithes - a proportion of the whole of the village tithes apportioned to the incumbent. The Greater Tithes were collected by the monarch or, in Houghton's case, someone appointed by him (William Chamberlain, The Earl of Gloucester, St Albans Abbey). As the incumbent received his share "vicariously", this was called a vicarage, and the incumbent was called a Vicar, as he is today.

# CHAPTER 4

## THE MAKING OF DUNSTABLE

William I had been a strong and efficient ruler, keeping "good peace", in the land; "Amongst other things the good security he made in this country is not to be forgotten - so that any honest man could travel over his kingdom without injury with his bosom full of gold; and no one dared strike (or kill) another..." as the Anglo Saxon Chronicles put it. Peaceful times of course helped the entrepreneurial leanings of the Houghton Regis farmers who traded at the crossroads.

On the death of William I, his eldest son Robert held Normandy, and the English crown came to his second son William Rufus (so called because of his red face and fiery temperament) in 1087.

William II had no interest in the country he had inherited, and frittered away his resources on fruitless wars against his eldest brother. So when William's younger brother Henry I succeeded him in 1100 it was to a much depleted royal purse, and still having to fend off the claims to the throne of brother Robert, Duke of Normandy.

Henry's advisers suggested that a market town built where the Icknield Way crossed Watling Street on his estate at Houghton Regis would be a good source of revenue. The profits from agricultural land were very dependant on good weather and other imponderables, but market towns provided a steady income from cash rents for houses, shops and market stalls, levies on trade, and the benefits of providing for travellers and traders alike.

Henry therefore offered building land to rent all round the crossroads. (He conveniently ignored the fact that William I had given the Kensworth quadrant to St Paul's Cathedral). These new tenants would be "burgesses" and therefore quite free to travel wherever they wished, buy and sell, and educate their sons or apprentice them as they liked. This was a freedom not accorded to the feudally bound farming tenants living in Houghton Regis who must have bitterly resented the newcomers' rights, since they could do none of those things without leave of the lord of the manor.

About 450 acres of Houghton land were used to build the market town with workshops and houses around three sides of the cross-roads, and to compensate for lost grazing ground, etc, the villagers were later given land at Buckwood (near Markyate).

However, the new town was built specifically as a market and business centre and did not really compete with the village for food production, so the King's estate must have profited from the increased market for local produce.

The King kept most of the south-west quadrant of the crossroads (East Street) for his own use, and had a royal residence built there. It was completed and furnished by 1109 and since it was large enough for formal Royal courts to be held there on occasion, must have been of considerable size.

The Royal household stayed at the new residence, called Kingsbury, in 1109 and during this visit it was probably the juxtaposition of two quite ordinary Royal events which had far reaching consequences for both

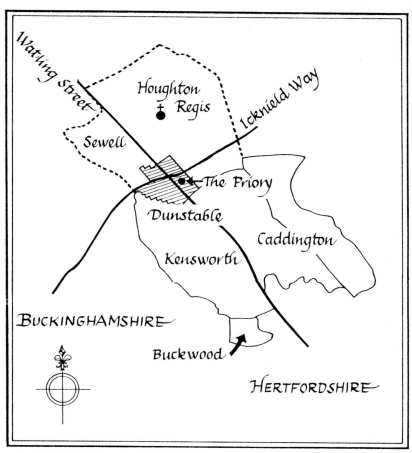

Fig. 4   A sketchmap showing the land allocated from Houghton
Regis to form Dunstable.    Buckwood is to the south.

Houghton and Dunstable.

Firstly, Queen Matilda had become interested in a
new religious order.  The parochial system as we know
it did not become generally established until late in
the twelfth century, and before that groups of clergy
(known as canons) often shared a communal house and
walked or rode about the nearby villages.  A group of
such canons at St Botolph's, Colchester, became
interested in following the 'rule' of St Augustine,

and later they adapted St Botolphs into an Augustinian House. During the royal visit to Dunstable, Henry signed a document allowing canons from St Bololph's to adapt Holy Trinity, Aldgate, into an Augustinian Priory, sponsored by Queen Matilda.

Also during this visit he would have inspected the new town and have heard complaints and petitions in the usual way from his Royal estate and from the new residents. A prospering new town needed a great deal of organisation and discipline.

Thinking over his discussions with the Queen, King Henry probably realized the advantages to his new town of having an Augustinian Priory nearby. The canons would all be clergy - educated men, who could run the town, represent him in important ways such as collecting his dues and taxes, and holding a manorial court. A priory would also provide suitable hospitality for travellers and a more convenient church.

He invited Bernard, one of the Brothers who had helped to found Aldgate Priory, to lead a group of canons and start an Augustinian house in Dunstable, on land opposite his palace.

The town of Dunstable flourished, as did the Priory. In 1130, Henry I gave the Priory "the whole manor and burg of Dunstaple" together with the town's land. He also gave the Priors common rights in the woods and pastures of Houghton, so the freemen of Houghton had to share their rights to Buckwood, given to them to compensate for the loss of land to make Dunstable, with the Priory! And, even worse, their pasture land had also to be shared. It was a very contentious gift indeed.

The Priory's charter also gave the Prior the sort of control over the town and its residents that the King had enjoyed when it was part of his demesne. This was in direct contradication of his original offer to businessmen who came to settle there. He had said that they would enjoy the kind of freedom and privileges that burgesses of London had. This dichotomy led to many disagreements in the future between the townspeople and the Prior.

As holder of the King's Charter in the town, and the landowner of a third of the village, the Prior had a major influence on local affairs.

The distinction between Dunstable and Houghton Regis was blurred until much more recent times. To begin with, the land had all been part of Houghton Regis and local people continued to think of it as such for a long time. The names of Upper Houghton and Dunstable were largely interchangeable, causing great confusion when it comes to working out relative population figures, etc. Many village people worked and owned property in Dunstable, and many townspeople farmed and owned land in Houghton.

Although the townspeople used the Priory for worship from the times of Henry I onwards, it was not until the dissolution of the monasteries under Henry VIII that Dunstable actually became a separate parish, with an area of nearly a square mile, and the Priory as its parish church.

The parish boundaries reflected the old area of the King's demesne until 1961 when the western side of Pointers Road became part of Dunstable parish, and the boundary was also moved from Union Street in Dunstable to the line of the old railway. As Father Blackburn remarks in his history of Houghton church, this was then considered to be a permanent way! Further rationalization of all local parish boundaries is currently being considered. They are being brought more into line with civil boundaries for fiscal and administrative convenience.

Fig. 5  This very old drawing shows the moat at Calcutt Farm before it was filled in, with the late 16th century farm building in the background.  (F.W.P.)

# CHAPTER 5

## THE DIVIDED LANDS

It was not so much the making of Dunstable which affected Houghton, it was Henry's division of the village between three major landlords.

1) He made the new town and gave the land plus a share of grazing and woods at Houghton to the Priory.

2) He gave the church lands of Houghton to his illegitimate son Robert Earl of Gloucester in 1121, and Robert gave them to St Albans Abbey in 1153.

3) He rented the village itself to a Norman baron, Hugh de Gurnay.

For the next 250 years, these three landlords and their descendants quarrelled incessantly over their respective pieces of land.

Hugh de Gurnay lived on the borders between Normandy and France, and was an absentee landlord in every sense of the word.  He and his descendants were in and out of favour with the current monarch with bewildering frequency.  Whenever the reigning English King thought that Hugh was being disloyal, he would take back Hugh's Houghton land and give it to the Prior.  When Hugh was once more in favour, back came his Houghton land again.  This happened every few years, until in King John's reign Hugh was fighting against the English and the Prior put his own staff into the manor house, north of the church, and claimed the whole village for the Priory.

This time when Hugh returned to favour, he politely asked the Prior to remove his men. The Prior refused, so Hugh sent armed men and demolished the house to its foundations. Hugh then built himself a new manor house at Thorn - the moat of this manor can still be seen on private ground.

The Prior was furious, and took the matter to the King's court at Westminster in 1223. The court tactfully awarded the Prior one third of all the woodland and meadow in the village (including one third of Buckwood). Surveyors went round and measured exactly which parts of each field and even parts of which tree belonged to the Prior. In addition, they awarded him a large enclosed farm towards Chalgrave called Caldecot. The land is on the map today as Calcutt Farm. In 1226 Prior Richard built his own manor house there and diverted a stream to make himself a moat, no doubt feeling that honour had been seen to be satisfied!

The village manor (often called "Thornbury" to distinguish it from Calcutt and from the church lands) passed through the de Gurnay family until about 1203, when the second Hugh de Gurnay left an under age heiress. William de Cantilupe, an official of King John, owned the manor of Eaton and he bought from John the right to administer the estate of de Gurnay's daughter and to arrange her marriage, thus linking Houghton and Eaton. It appears that the daughter married first Almaric, Count of Evreux and, when he died, William de Cantilupe himself.

In 1254 William's son (or grandson) inherited, and as he was a minor, both villages (Eaton and Houghton) were run by royal officials. The boy died aged 21 in

1273. His sister, who inherited both villages, was married to Eudo la Zouche.

Trouble flared again between the Priory and the la Zouches in 1274, when "John the Cook", who was a tenant of the Prior, was accused of theft at Eudo's village court. Because he was a Calcutt tenant, the Prior wanted the fine, and had him removed to his prison at Calcutt.

Late on the night of June 9th, Eudo and Millicent sent a knight and armed men to Calcutt where they broke open the Prior's prison and carried off John to their own gaol. This unfortunate felon was later sent to prison at Bedford where he died!

This kidnapping sparked off a whole new series of quarrels about shared grazing and boundaries. Eudo took the Prior to court. The Prior offered to make amends, but not in court, so Eudo's men refused to let the Prior use any of the Houghton grazing land. They took 24 of the Prior's draught horses which were grazing on their shared pastures, and shut them up until they starved to death. Without horses, of course, the canons could not plough the land that year, and were desperately short of bread.

The final insult before these two landlords eventually patched up their quarrels, was when Eudo's men went one night and destroyed the Prior's gallows which were set up in a field south of the old "Edeway".

Not only are there records of successive lords of the manor quarrelling with the Priory, but the third landowner, St Albans Abbey, and the chief, free tenants of the village all seem to have engaged in constant squabbling.

As holders of the church and church lands from 1153 to the dissolution of the monasteries, St Albans Abbey collected tithes from the whole village (except Calcutt) - one tenth of everything the villagers grew, made or collected - and the church lands were farmed by the Abbey steward.

We can see how wily and high-handed the village landlords were by a list of grievances drawn up by a jury of Houghton men to be presented to the royal justices at the end of the 13th Century. They complained that:-

1. The men of Houghton had freely let their land to the men of Dunstable until one year there had been a disagreement between them. William de Cantilupe as lord of the manor, had impounded the Dunstable crops until each man had paid a fine of 12d, and from then on, he charged each Dunstablian 12d anyway, as an annual ground rent! As a result, many of them went elsewhere to look for land so that the Houghton farmers suffered by the loss of rents.

2. The villagers had always been fined 10s if they failed to attend their landlord's main court. This was acceptable practice, but suddenly, without warning, the 10s was made a mandatory payment as 'rent' and there was an additional fine for absence!

3. Robbery and murder of strangers (travellers) was quite common and Houghton had two main road boundaries. If the village failed to produce the murderer, they had to share the fine paid to compensate the King for loss of a subject. (For example, when John Spongebelles' two-horse cart ran over a boy and killed him, the family received

nothing, but the compensation payable to the King was 6s8d). When the King's Justice met at Dunstable in 1227, the death of three strangers (travellers) was reported. The total fine was 100s but the Prior's share of 8s for Calcutt (church land) was excused. However, he was then given two large pieces of secular land in the village, yet, when there was a murder fine of £5 to pay, the Prior still refused to contribute.

4.  John of Casterton, Millicent Cantilupe's steward, was responsible for her widely scattered estates and in 1283, as the harvest was late at Houghton, he was anxious to move on and check the winter stores elsewhere. He asked the villagers to bring forward the date of the main court or to cut the corn early. They refused because their neighbours, who were away trading, would have no notice and be fined for absence. They were also worried in case if they agreed once, he would change the date every year. But Casterton promised that there would be no precedent set, and no fines incurred. So the court was held, and when it ended, he fined all the absentees!

The Prior held his own court at Calcutt, and the tenants of the church land had to attend the Abbot's court. The sort of matters dealt with in these manor courts were:

- a list made and fines levied on all absentees
- enquiries started concerning any serious crimes such as murder, homicide and burglary, or

misdemeanours such as theft, receiving
stolen goods, harbouring strangers,
keeping treasure trove.
- farming offences such as blocking or
diverting brooks, paths or roads.
- trading offences such as using false
measures or selling bread or beer
above the price set by the land owner.

A record was kept of all matters to come before the
courts, and for a fee anyone could look up exactly
what the "custom" of the manor was --- that is, what
had been decided in the past over any particular
matter, such as a land dispute and use this to help
argue his case.

The courts may have been strict, but they do seem
to have been fair, and public, and to have offered the
villagers of Houghton, as elsewhere, some check on
their landlord's general highhandedness.

# CHAPTER 6

## CIVIL WAR

Reports of damage done to the neighbourhood, the involvement and sentiments of Houghton landowners and other circumstancial evidence show us how Houghton was affected by the Civil War which took place during King John's reign.

When Richard I (1189-1199) was abroad on the Third Crusade, England was left in the hands of administrators occupied with their own quarrels. Richard himself sold everything that he could - land, manors, earldoms and various other posts - to raise money for the Crusade. Meanwhile his brother John was plotting against him at home, until Richard died of a poisoned battle wound and John in his turn became King.

He seems to have alienated nearly everyone. He quarrelled with the Pope, and this resulted in the Interdict of 1208-1214, which meant that people were forbidden to use their church - they could not be married, buried, baptised or even attend mass in church during all this period. Such ceremonies as there were took place in the churchyard. King John raised heavy taxes to pay for his unsuccessful wars in France, despite which he lost most of the huge empire built up by his father Henry II.

At home, he rode roughshod over the barons, until, reluctantly, they rebelled against him. In order to

Fig. 6    King John's Seal.

quell them John employed mercenary soldiers, one of
the most successful being a Norman called Falkes de
Breauté, who was both loyal to King John and a
powerful fighter.

In 1213 the Barons, Church leaders and civic
representatives from the royal towns (including
Dunstable) met at St Albans Abbey and planned the
Magna Carta.  This was an important document setting
out rights and protective clauses for all free men.
Its fundamental and inheritable rights have stood in
law to this day.

The following year, the northern barons met
together and marched to Bedford Castle where they met
up with William de Beauchamp and marched south to
challenge the King.

King John, however, resorted to endless delaying tactics, and even when finally obliged to sign the Manga Carta in June 1215, he constantly ignored it and the rebellion continued.

Unfortunately Houghton, Dunstable and the surrounding countryside were in the path of the opposing forces who marched through the area on numerous occasions, and local landowners were heavily involved on one side or the other.

King John himself stayed overnight at the Priory in 1216 while his troops camped throughout the neighbourhood. Medieval armies lived off the land, taking whatever food and other goods they needed in passing and there is no doubt that the Houghton farms would have been stripped bare. On the opposing side, the Earl of Perche (whose property at Toddington had been siezed by John in 1205) marched along Watling Street with the Marshall of France and 1000 French soldiers on his way to support the barons. The Earl did protect the Priory, but the soldiers damaged buildings and churches outside the town as well as helping themselves to whatever they needed on their way through. As time went on and parties from both sides passed along the main roads, the marauding soldiers would, of course, have had to penetrate further and further into the countryside to find the food and supplies they needed, and no doubt the actual village of Houghton also suffered.

The political scene had been further complicated by the arrival of Prince Louis of France. The barons had invited him to become King of England in place of John and he had disembarked on the Kent coast with his French army in the May of 1216. Henry Marshall Junior supported Prince Louis and thereby forfeited the manor of Luton to Falkes de Breaute, making this fearsome mercenary a very close and uncomfortable neighbour. Falkes had already been given Bedford Castle after capturing it from William de Beauchamp.

King John died on October 18th 1216, leaving the nine year old Henry (III) as King. Falkes de Breauté and William Marshall Senior were John's executors. William Marshall who had been a loyal supporter of both Henry II and King John, now became Regent of all England. He reissued the Magna Carta and promised it would be effective. William de Cantilupe (of Houghton and Eaton), William Marshall Junior and many others agreed to support the young king.

However, Prince Louis and his French troops were still in England, and too many outrages had been committed by both sides for peace to come straight away. On separate occasions Prince Louis and Falkes de Breauté both attacked St Albans Abbey and the town of St Albans demanding money with menaces, and in Falkes de Breauté's case, committing murder actually in the Abbey. Meanwhile, throughout the area, the warring factions continued to steal food, oxen, horses and carts so that civilian food supplies nearly came to a standstill.

In May 1217, Prince Louis and his men were besieged in Lincoln Castle. William Marshall Senior had been unable to take the castle, but when he arrived, Falkes de Breauté managed to force a back entry and with his men stood on the parapets and dropped heavy stones onto the horses in the castle yard below. In the confusion, the main party broke in and William de Beauchamp of Bedford was taken prisoner. There was a terrible massacre as the French troops poured out of the castle and were trapped between the two armies of Falkes de Breaute and William Marshall. Inside the castle the Earl of Perche stubbornly fought on until William Marshall had to kill him in order to end the affair.

This battle, with its terrible losses, ended Prince Louis' claim to the throne and marked the end of the Civil War. Louis and the remnants of his army retreated across country. They camped around our area and the men, desperate for food, supplies and money, once again robbed and terrorized the neighbourhood, even damaging the Priory, before they retreated to the coast.

Although the rest of the country was now peaceful, Houghton, Dunstable and Luton were in a miserable position.

Falkes de Breauté had built himself a castle at Luton from which he harried the whole of the neighbourhood. His crack troops were no longer needed in these peaceful times and were kicking their heels in enforced idleness and having to be both fed and kept. Raiding parties plagued the neighbourhood. Each week, when Houghton farmers took their produce into Dunstable they risked meeting Falkes de Breauté's men who regarded the market as their source of free supplies!

William de Cantilupe was so worried about the safety of his property at Eaton and Houghton that he built a 'castle' at Eaton (Bray). It was a defended manor house with an outer bailey big enough to stable 60 horses. The annalist at Dunstable Priory seems to have regarded both this castle and that of Falkes de Breaute with an equally jaundiced eye.

Falkes de Breauté had, of course, been a great hero and had been loyal to both King John and then Henry III, but in the end the young King could not ignore the misery being caused to his subjects. Falkes de Breauté had failed to attend the King's Court at Bedford so he was summoned to appear before the King's Itinerant Justices at Dunstable Priory. If he refused, he was likely to be outlawed.

The people of Luton brought many charges of stolen land and of houses pulled down when he built his castle. Houghton's third landlord, the Abbot of St. Albans, complained of damaged crops and a ruined watermill on his Luton land, caused by the diversion of the River Lea when Falkes dug out his moat.

However, Falkes did not attend the Court, he stayed away on the Welsh borders, but his brother William rode out from Bedford Castle to kidnap the Judges! Two of them escaped, but the third, Henry de Braybroc, rode into a trap and was borne off to the dungeons of Bedford Castle.

Henry de Braybroc's wife Christiana rode to Northampton and begged the King for help.

This time, Falkes had gone too far. The King could not ignore this flaunting of his authority. Messengers were sent to demand that Falkes should come to Bedford, while King Henry himself prepared to besiege Bedford Castle and rescue the Judge. The aggrieved people of Dunstable (which probably included Calcutt and Upper Houghton), were given the somewhat doubtful privilege of leading the attack and gaining spoils of horses, harness, oxen, crossbows and "countless other plunder". Many died on both sides during the siege.

Eventually, eighty of Falkes' men were hanged and the rest dispersed, much to the relief of the people of Houghton and Dunstable I should think! Falkes de Breaute himself was outlawed and, two years later in 1226, died from eating a poisoned fish supper at St Ciriac in France.

Falkes gave his name to a part of London. He married Margaret de Rivers, a wealthy widow, who owned the land where he built his manor house 'Falkes Hall', recorded as Faukes-Hale in 1279 and now known as Vauxhall. In 1857 Alexander Wilson started the Vauxhall Iron Works on this land, building the first Vauxhall car there in 1903 and bringing the name back to Luton in 1905. The griffin used as the Vauxhall trademark is based on Falkes' personal standard. The

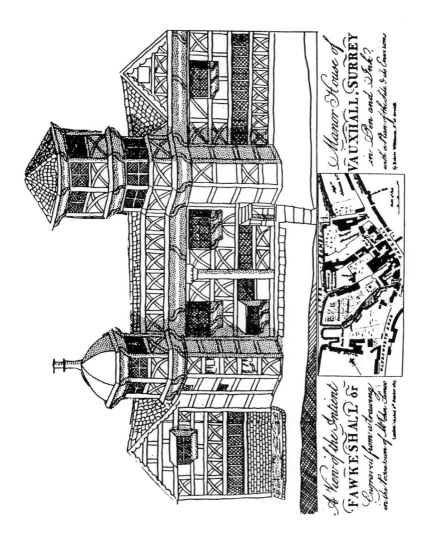

Fig. 7   Faukes-Hale (Falkes' Hall) from a drawing published in 1813.

Fig. 8    The Vauxhall griffin. (V.M.L.)

Dunstable factory is within the original Houghton parish boundaries, and has provided a livelihood for many modern Houghton residents ever since.

# CHAPTER 7

## REBUILDING THE CHURCH

Robert, Earl of Gloucester may well have given the old Saxon church a major overhaul, or even largely rebuilt it when he rebuilt St Mary's, Luton, or perhaps it was repaired or replaced piecemeal until the present church was built in the 13th/14th Century.

Not only is the history of the Saxon church swathed in mystery, but nowhere is there any record of when the present building replaced the original church, or of who was responsible for building it.

If St Albans Abbey had rebuilt the church themselves they would have recorded it, and there is no such record in their main accounts. Many Abbey documents of this period were however damaged by fire in the 18th Century and it may well be that there is some clue there which techniques yet to be invented will enable future historians to discover.

If Dunstable Priory had rebuilt the church, they too would have recorded it and would never have allowed St Albans Abbey to reap the benefits as the two were constantly squabbling!

It is interesting to note that William de Cantilupe bought Eaton (Bray) in the early 13th century and he paid for the Eaton church of St Mary the Virgin to be rebuilt. He intended this to be of a very grand and

Fig. 9    A conjectural drawing of the 13th/14th century church.

ornate design, and it is thought that Abbot John de
Cella of St. Albans Abbey advised him in the work.
The church had actually been given to Merton Priory by
William's predecessor, and William is thought to have
quarrelled with the Prior before rebuilding was
finished and to have stopped work on it because of
this.

   William was obviously interested in church
architecture and it may be that the de Cantilupe
(later La Zouche) family rebuilt All Saints, Houghton
Regis, as lords of the manor, prodded on by St Albans
Abbey. We may never know.

   From the architectural style of the church, however,
we know  that the main parts (the chancel, nave and
aisles) were built in the 13th/14th Century in the
decorated style of English architecture.   The roof
would have been steeply pitched over the nave; in
fact, the old line of the roof can clearly be seen on
the outside of the tower's eastern wall, together with
the shape of a doorway which would have led to a roof
space.   It many have been a thatched roof, or covered
with wooden shingles and the roof would have carried
on over the aisles in some way.   This original
building would have looked rather plain.

Fig. 10

The arch of the main door is 14th
century.  The heads either side
are said to be of the Archbishop
of Canterbury and the Bishop of
Lincoln of the time.

The main doorway is 14th Century (although it has
been restored) but it would not have had the present
porch, which is thought to have been built in the
15th/16th Century.  The heads on the mouldings by the
door are said to be of the Archbishop of Canterbury
and the Bishop of Lincoln of the time.

The outer walls have been rebuilt and later style
windows inserted, but inside the original 14th Century
arcades remain.  They make five bays and have huge
octagonal pillars with moulded capitals and bases.

On one of the main pillars  on the north side of
the aisle is scratched the shape of a bird. This is
thought to be the sign of a group of medieval pilgrims
who left their mark in each church as they passed,
each group using its own individual sign.

Originally there was a figure of a saint standing
on a bracket set into each pillar.  The saints
represented were the Blessed Virgin, Anne, Anthony,
Christopher, Clement, John, Katherine, Margaret, Mary
Magdelene, Michael, Nicholas, Swithin and Thomas.  The
figures were largely bequests from local wills.  One
of the brackets supporting the figure can still be
seen on the eastern pillar of the south side (for a

Fig. 11   The main pillars and bays are 14th century, as is the
          chancel arch.

long time it proved very useful for supporting the
hymn-board!)   and this is thought to have been the
bracket for the Virgin Mary.

Behind the organ is a 14th Century piscina (a
drained basin usually set in the wall near an altar).

The present plain decoration and open chancel of
the church give very little idea of what the building
would have looked like originally.   The statues and
ornamentation would have been gilded and painted, much
richer in colour and detail.   The rood screen would
have been much heavier in design and would effectively
have cut off the nave from the chancel, where mass was
largely celebrated away from the congregation.

There would almost certainly have been a highly
decorative Rood: a   representation of the Cross above
the rood screen between the nave and the chancel.
Sometimes these representations were life-size or
bigger and housed in a rood loft.   This could be

42

Fig. 12
The Norman font, the work of a group
of Totternhoe font makers.

something like six feet deep with statues of Christ on
the Cross flanked by the Virgin Mary and St John and
perhaps giving room for a few singers and a priest to
read the Gospel.  The whole thing would have been
colourful and dramatic in concept.

From the outside of the church a blocked doorway
can be seen in the north aisle level with the rood
screen.  This may have been the entrance to a former
vestry, or it may have been an entrance to a rood
loft.

The chancel was originally early 14th Century, but
had to be rebuilt on its ancient foundations in 1879.
The rear arches and some of the jambs (the main
central pillars) of the windows were used in the
reconstruction together with much of the old material.
The arch into the chancel is original.

The 14th Century church would have had at least one
reminder of the original building which can be seen,
and is regularly used, today; and this is the
beautiful Norman font in the south aisle.  It is a
very fine example of the work of a group of Totternhoe
font makers.  Houghton babies have been baptised in it
over the last 750 years or so, with much the same
feelings of parental pride, no doubt, then as now.

# CHAPTER 8

## FAMINE AND PLAGUE

During the 13th century as a whole, England was going through a period of exceptionally favourable climate, and this was particularly important to a largely agricultural community such as Houghton. The harvests were heavy and the quality of the corn good, which meant better food, fewer deaths and a rising population.

The tax assessment for Houghton in 1297 is lost, but that for Dunstable shows it to be a prosperous place, with many varied trades represented and many shops selling food. The town and its visitors would have been a ready market for Houghton produce of all kinds, so we can be sure that Houghton was prospering too.

In 1309 the tax assessment shows that although Houghton had 60% less population than Dunstable, it paid only 50% less taxes. Houghton also had nearly twice the taxable population of other villages in Bedfordshire.

There then followed, however, a spell when the climate which had been favourable for so long reverted to normal unpredictable cold and wet spells; agriculture deteriorated and the population shrank. The winter of 1314 was cold and wet, producing a poor harvest, and poor quality seed corn for 1315. There was virtually no harvest in 1315 and a state of famine followed which was nation wide. Imported corn did not reach the general public, it was snatched by the King (Edward II) and put on the black market.

In 1317, "murain" (possibly foot and mouth disease) caused cows and pigs to drop dead in the field so that their carcasses could not be used for food.

Medieval agriculture, once damaged, took decades to recover, especially on poor chalk soil such as that of most of Houghton. A weakened population with no powered machinery and neglected land, only led to more weak and sickly people.

Added to these natural calamities, there were heavy taxes to pay for the King's unsuccessful war in France. This was the Hundred Years' War, which was more a long series of expensive skirmishes, with the protagonists withdrawing from time to time as their countries became virtually bankrupt. Soldiers were 'called up' to fight in France, reducing still further the number of men able to work the land.

By 1340 things were so bad that when the tax collectors came to Houghton they found that the population had fallen, the land was uncultivated, and the people impoverished. They had "neither seed to sow, nor oxen to plough."

Despite the prevailing gloom, Edward III seems to have been fond of tournaments and chivalrous gestures. In 1342 Dunstable was chosen for a tournament to celebrate a great naval victory at Sluys where the French fleet had been destroyed. Nigel Loring of Chalgrave had played a prominent part in the victory, which gave England mastery of the Channel for the next 30 years. Local tournaments may have been held on the land at the western end of the parish where the sewage farm now is. The tournaments were banned during periods of political unrest but at other times attracted huge crowds and brought extra visitors and more trade, as well as an unwelcome element of violence, theft and hooliganism.

In 1346 soldiers were called up from all over Bedfordshire to fight in France and rumours began to circulate about a terrible disease raging on the continent which left "whole towns dead and no one to bury them." The following year, the Black Death hit the area.

The annalist at Dunstable Priory does not record the number of local deaths, but some idea of the intensity of the plague can be judged by the fact that at St Albans 75% of the monks died.

Between 33% and 50% of the population in England died during the Black Death and we can assume that at Houghton, as elsewhere, other people were left too weak to work during the next farming year. The harvest of 1348 probably seeded and rotted in the fields, and it is possible that it was 10-15 years before the open fields were once again fully cultivated. Livestock probably roamed the countryside uncared for and unmilked. When the plough oxen were killed in 1066, the countryside had not recovered 20 year later; once again recovery would have been a slow process.

Economists and historians consider that the severity of the Black Death was aggravated by weakness and malnutrition and that the high death rate was the result of several diseases attacking at the same time.

It certainly resulted in far reaching changes of land ownership and tenanacy. Previously lords and landowners could bully peasants into submission with threats of homelessness and starvation, since the workers were tied to their lord's service and often could not leave the manor without his permission. Furthermore they had had to provide him with obligatory work-days, that is, free labour. After the Black Death, however, labour was short and the land workers could demand not only a secure roof over their heads, but also a reasonable wage.

Villeins (tied agricultural workers) who survived, often had the chance to take on 'free land' or to rent strips adjoining their own, thus improving their holdings. They no longer wanted the drudgery of obligatory work-days for the landlord and took the opportunity to try to commute these into cash payments. If a worker wanted to leave one master and offer his services to another, retribution was not as certain as it had been -- many landlords were not above poaching when labour was so short. Gradually a new sort of farmer emerged, a man free to work his own land, renting that land for money and supplying only an agreed amount of produce to the manor.

Religious houses, however, refused to give "free" tenancies to their farms, and some villeins ran away and tried to hide in the towns or to join more liberal estates where they would not be bound absolutely to the landlord. Some were caught and returned but others remained free.

We do not have any information on this specific to Houghton, but with three separate lords of the manor, two of them religious houses, we can be sure that the situation was troubled and confused in the village as elsewhere.

The Statute of Labourers, passed in 1351 imposed a "wage freeze", penalizing employers who tried to reach private agreements with landworkers. Prices continued to rise, however.

Despite the misery of his people, Richard II, who had succeeded King Edward, imposed even more heavy taxes, including a "poll" or head tax which meant that the larger a family, the higher the taxes it had to

pay.   Unpopular laws were passed which tried to
inhibit the movement of labour and the country still
struggled with the aftermath of famine and plague.
These and other pressures led to the Peasants' Revolt
of 1381.

When the young King Richard, in London, was faced
with a mob of rebels made up of deputations from
different parts of England, he promised them that he
personally would be responsible for righting their
wrongs.  The crowds dispersed, but as soon as the
rebels were safely disbanded, the King's soldiers
overtook them.  Locally, a court was held in St Albans
where several of the ringleaders were hanged.

It was the annalist at St Albans who coined the
name "Peasants'" revolt, using the term perjoratively,
but the people who revolted locally were mainly tenant
farmers and businessmen.  In Houghton, they would have
included tenants of the religious houses.

Houghton Regis is not mentioned by name, but all
the evidence suggests that Houghton men took an active
part.  The tenant farmers from Calcutt led by Thomas
Hobbes, land lord of the Swan Inn in Upper Houghton,
joined the businessmen from Dunstable who stormed the
gates of the Priory.  Both the Abbot at St Albans
(also faced with a threatening mob) and the Prior each
granted a new charter, but when the revolt had been
suppressed both charters were taken back.

Seeds of caution were sown, however: the poll tax
was dropped.  Gradually, the power of the religious
houses began to wane, and in the countryside, the
yeoman farmer had appeared, making a rural middle
class between the peasantry and the lord of the manor.
It was a time of great change.

## CHAPTER 9

## 15TH CENTURY IMPROVEMENTS

Eventually the bitterness of 1381 died down and as the power of the religious houses faded farmers, businessmen and landlords settled down together.

The men living in High Street North and Upper Houghton commuted to London and joined the livery companies. There was a period of great prosperity; so many travellers flocked up and down Watling Street that the Prior was obliged to license the building of more inns, and there was work for anyone producing or selling food and goods for men and horses.

The decline in the power of the religious houses also meant that social responsibility gradually shifted to members of the community. Local wills now provided not only for the saying of prayers for the soul of the deceased, but also for the upkeep of the church, repair of local roads and care of the poor.

Wealthy businessmen got together in towns to form fraternities or brotherhoods whose purposes were religious, charitable and also often social. The Luton Fraternity of the Holy Trinity, part of whose beautifully illuminated register is in Luton Museum, contains the name of many Houghton men and women, together with the date of their enrolment.

John Fossy                                              1476
Thomas Norette & Joan his wife of Howghton    1504

Harry Page & Robert Page & Eliz. his wife
of Hogthorn

Alice Norrat of Howghton                          1516
John Eme & Alice his wife
John Barbour & Joan                               1517
John Hawkyns & Marion his wife of Howghton
Richard Wallis & Joan his wife of Howghton
William Perott & Joan his wife of Howghton
Margaret Smyth                                    1521
William Fosce, bat.
Sir Henry Barker.  John & Alice
father & mother         1522
Richard Webbe and Julian
Richard Wylde                                     1523
Sir William Fosse, Vicar                          1524
William Smyth
Margaret Fosse
Mathew Pedder
Thomas Mele
John Hamond, bat.                                 1524
John Smyth, bat.
Richard Wylde, bat.
Thomas Fowler & Sybel his wife                    1525
William Strang & Alice his wife                   1527
Thomas Hardynge & Eliz                            1529
Joan Pedder
William Lyen, bat.                                1530
Robert Hawkyns & Eliz                             1533
Nicholas Fonten                                   1535
Thomas Barbor
John Eyme & Agnes                                 1537
John Colman & Margaret
Thomas Ympee & Anne

These family names are of interest not least
because so many of them are still to be found in the
neighbourhood.

Sir William Fosse was in fact vicar of All Saints,
Houghton Regis in 1524 (the title Sir was a courtesy
title of the clergy, as Reverend is now, and does not

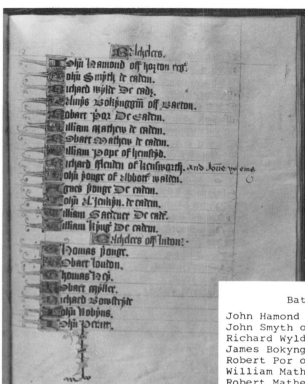

f. 76

Batchelors

John Hamond of Houghton Regis
John Smyth of the same
Richard Wylde of the same
James Bokynggm of Barton
Robert Por of the same
William Mathew of the same
Robert Mathew of the same
William Pope of Hempstead
Richard fflenden of Kensworth
  (and Joan his wife - added)
John Yonge of Abbots Walden
Agnes Yonge of the same
John a Jenkyn of the same
William Gardener of the same
William Kyng of the same

Batchelors of Luton

Thomas Yonge
Robert London
Thomas Hey
Robert Myller
Richard Bowftryde
John Robyns
John Peratt

Fig. 13    A page of the Register of the Luton Fraternity of the
           Holy Trinity . (L.M.)

51

Fig. 14    The interior of the 15th century tithe barn demolished
in 1964.  (C.R.O.)

Fig. 15    The exterior of the tithe barn with the church on the
left and the first houses of Tithe Farm Estate on the
right. (C.R.O.)

necessarily imply knighthood).

The object of this Guild was to maintain a priest and to care for poor members. Mass was sung for the "good estate" of the brethren (and sisters) while living and for the repose of their souls after death. The Fraternity chaplains were paid an average of 2s7d for saying a dirge on the death of a brother or sister.

The Prior of Dunstable was still a major landowner in the village, and the church lands still belonged to St Albans Abbey.

A reminder of the 15th Century which remained until the present Tithe Farm Estate was built, was a huge barn which stood on the site of the present Youth Centre. It is thought to have been built by Abbot John Moore (1396-1401) when the Abbey chronicles record "a good grange on a foundation of stone, of timber and earth, well tiled and enclosed...... with a strong wall." The barn was demolished in 1964 because the timbers were too rotten to be preserved.

Thornbury, Houghton village manor, passed through the family of la Zouche until 1485. In 1483 John la Zouche fought with the unsuccessful Richard II at the Battle of Bosworth and as a result lost his lands. The village manor was then administered by the crown for five years until in 1490 Henry VII granted Houghton and Eaton (Bray) to Sir Reginald de Bray.

Sir Reginald de Bray was an important politician of his time who became High Treasurer and Chancellor of the Duchy of Lancaster. He was also a famous architect who helped to design St George's Chapel at Windsor, and the Henry VII Chapel at Westminster Abbey. Nearer home, he completed the work which de Cantiloupe had started at St Mary the Virgin at Eaton Bray.

Once again there is no evidence as to who was responsible for work done at All Saints, Houghton Regis, during this period. The architectural style indicates the fifteenth century or thereabouts, and it is interesting to note that Sir Reginald de Bray was lord of the manor of both Houghton and Eaton at this time when many alterations were made to the church building to make it bigger, grander and lighter.

The tower was added in the 15th century. It is in three stages, and houses six bells. One mounts to the original stages or floors by a winding stair-turret in the south-west corner, but fortunately a floor added in recent years has a less demanding inside staircase.

Looking at the tower from outside, there are two niches either side of the main window. They would each have housed the figure of a saint, but the Saints have long ago succumbed to iconoclasm or the weather. Only the outer part of the main window is original.

Inside the tower are six bells of different dates inscribed:

1st Bell
JOHN BRIANT HERTFORD FECIT                                    1815

2nd Bell
J. BRIANT HERTFORD FECIT                                      1816

3rd Bell
NEWCOMBE MADE MEE                                             1616
Recast Taylor                                                1819

4th Bell
J. BRIANT HERTFORD FECIT                                      1811

5th Bell
O.B. JOHN DIER MADE ME                                       1580
Recast Taylor                                                1899

Fig. 16    The 15th century church building with tower and
clerestory windows.

6th Bell
ANTHONY CHANDLER MADE MEE                              1673

The fifth is thought to be the earliest dated bell
in Bedfordshire.

Apparently in 1552 the number of bells had been
increased from four to five, but went back to the
original number because the fifth bell could not be
paid for and had to be sold!

After the tower was built the roof of the nave was
raised to its present position in order to allow
clerestory windows to be put in above the roof level
of the aisles and at the same time the pitch of the
roof was altered.    It no longer needed to be so
steeply pitched to throw off rain, since lead had now
been introduced as a roof covering instead of thatch
or wooden shingles.  Lead had an unfortunate tendency
to "creep" down a steep slope, so for this reason also
a gentler pitch was needed.

The use of lead meant that the outside appearance
of the church was transformed.  The old steep roof had
projected over the eaves to throw the rainwater clear

Fig. 17    Two of the 15th century gargoyles housing the spouts which threw rainwater clear of the walls.

Fig. 18    Two of the carved wooden angels which are part of the original 15th century nave roof.

of the walls, but the new flatter pitched roof had a gutter along the edge, behind a battlemented parapet, and the rainwater was thrown clear through spouts placed at intervals. The spouts were housed in gargoyles - fanciful stone creatures with rainwater erupting through their mouths.

Houghton church now had parapets not only on the tower but all along the church walls, with an interesting and varied series of gargoyles at intervals, all features which can still be seen.

The clerestory windows made the inside of the church much lighter and gave an appearance of greater space. Looking up from the nave it is possible to see the carved wooden angels which were part of the original 15th century roof. Some of them bear shields, some are empty handed, but undoubtedly each originally held an object. It is just possible to detect traces of gilding which must have made a blaze of colour against the dark wood.

There are four differently patterned panels in the eastern bay of the roof. They are ribbed with carved bosses and they would have formed a ceiling over the rood. The bosses and ribbing are original.

Just below the wooden roof can be seen the original carved corbel stones. These are supporting blocks bonded into the wall. The medieval craftsman took every opportunity to embellish the mundane necessities of building, and so each one has a creature of some sort carved on it.

The rood screen which stretches across the entrance to the chancel, is 15th century. Originally, it would have had folding doors in the central arch, since the chancel and the nave were separated. The congregation largely watched the celebration of mass from the nave through the upper part of the screen rather than participating in it as they do now.

Fig. 19    15th century corbel stones (supporting blocks bonded into the wall).

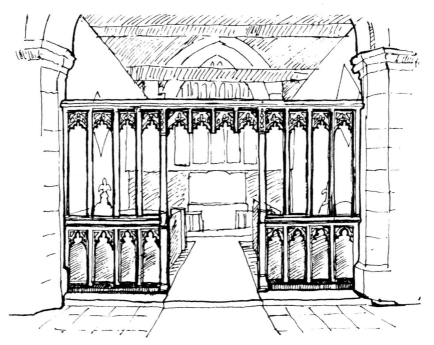

Fig. 20    The 15th century rood screen.

In the floor of the chancel can be seen part of a brass showing an effigy in Mass vestments with an inscription to John Waleys, Vicar 1410, and to his kinsman whose effigy was also originally shown, but is now lost.

In the south aisle is a recessed tomb. It has the arms of the Sewell family on it, and the figure is wearing armour of the mid 14th/early 15th century. The tomb appears to be Tudor, however, as it has panels of quatrefoil circles round a Tudor rose. It is thought to be an effigy of Sir John Sewell, one of the de Sewell family.

Fig. 21    The recessed tomb thought to house the effigy of Sir John Sewell.    The details of carving shown are the Tudor rose, and the lion at his feet, signifying that he died in battle.

Sewell paid a ground rent to the owner of Houghton. The tenancy remained separate from Houghton Regis even though it was put back into the main manor; Sewell was of course listed separately in the Domesday Book. Parts of the present manor house are believed to date back to the 12th Century.

The de Sewell family lived at Sewell all through the 13th, 14th and 15th century, until the last heiress married Edmund Dyve of Bromley and the family name thus changed to "Dyve." An ancestor, Adam de Sewell, was vicar of All Saints in 1329.

Fig. 22    Sewell Manor House as it appears today. (J.B.)

# CHAPTER 10

## SIXTEENTH CENTURY WILLS & THE FRATERNITY OF JESUS

In 1515 Houghton was made a very rich chantry bequest by William Dyve of Sewell. William was a wealthy businessman. Some time after 1500, he had gone to live in London, but he had not forgotten his native village. He or his family had bought the Swan Inn (Red Lion) on the corner of Church Street Dunstable, the Kings Head (White Horse) and most of the houses on the north side of Church Street down to Kingsbury; he used these and several pieces of land in Houghton to benefit the people of Sewell and Houghton after his death.

The income from the properties was to provide
. an extra priest for the manor chapel at Sewell
. an extra priest to be attached to All Saints Church to sing masses for his family
. money to be given to poor people to pray for his soul
. money to help poor people pay their taxes. In addition
. the priest at All Saints was to teach six poor children.

The school, the priest's house and the various properties of the endowment, known as the Fraternity of Jesus, are identified as being in Church Street by the rent list of 1542. The school was very roughly where Ashton St Peter's is now and it ran successfully for a number of years.

Houghton was one of only a handful of schools in all Bedfordshire. At that time, only wealthy people could afford to send their sons away to be educated, and there were few schools available for less wealthy people who wanted to educate their children.

The teacher lived near the school and was paid 26/8d per year.

Chantries were so called because they provided for a priest to chant or sing Mass for the soul of the departed and for his/her family. Under Edward VI they were all closed, but Edward's civil servants were so pleased with the Houghton "grammar" school that the teacher, John Couper, was paid to go on teaching there even though the King took away the Swan Inn and the rest of the endowment. The intention was that Couper should be paid £6 a year, and that the school should continue indefinitely, but payments only continued until 1555 when they stopped, possibly because Couper had died. Whatever the reason, Dyve school closed after running for 40 years.

The dissolution of the chantries pre-empted another part of William Dyve's will. He had put the endowments for the school into the hands of trustees for 99 years, and then if the King refused to grant a licence for the school to continue, they were to be sold and used to provide ornaments and repairs to the church.

However, he also provided for the mending of a road known as Pynder's Hill, for the marriages of "poor maidens" of Houghton, and for the relief of the poor, etc.

In this way, William's will reflected the provisions of many wills of the period. Civic responsibilities were devolving more and more from the religious houses to the community as a whole.

Primarily, wills tended to provide a sort of insurance for the well being of the departed's soul, and often provided for Masses to be said both for the departed and for his family. Lights (candles) were seen as maintaining a chain of prayer:

> "to the lights in the church of Houghton a cake of wax of 10 1b" (The will of Wm. Walle, vicar of Houghton Regis, died in 1506/7) .

> "To the high altar for tithes forgotten 1 bush wheat; to the All Hallows light in the chancel 1 bush. barley; to the rood light and Our Blessed Lady light 1 bush. barley each; to those of St. Nich and St. Martin 1 bush. and St. Thos and St. Margaret 1 bush; to the church 1 qtr malt; to the friars of Dunstable 1 qtr malt; to the torches (lamps) 2 bush. barley; his executors to cause a trental to be said in Houghton Regis church". (Will of Jn. How, died 1503).

This will gives us a good idea of just how many statues and consequently candles there were in the church at the time:

> "To the high altar 20d and 1 bush. wheat at Michaelmas; to the rood light 4d and those of Our Lady 4d, St Martin 2d, St. Margaret, St. Kath. and Mary Magdalene 2d, St. Thos and Our Lady of Pity 2d, St. Nich 2d, the 12 apostles 2d and all others in the church 1d". (Will of Agnes Smith, Houghton Regis, died 1503/4).

This good lady was evidently anxious not to offend any of the saints in the world to come!

She also had a good memory, for her will continues "Jn Webbe oweth her 6s8d which he is to keep"!

Richard Webbe's will (Houghton Regis, died 1506) mentions lights to all the above saints and in addition "St. Anne, St. Clement, St. Mich, St. William, St. Anthony, St. Chris, St. Jn and St. Sythe (Swithun)".

Alsone Margery of Houghton Regis (died 1499/1500) requested that his -- or is it her? -- body should be buried in the "chirchyarde of Howghton a for saide" and bequeathed 3s4d to the "chirch". William Fossey of "Kingeshoughton" (died 1524) left wax lights and £6.13.4d to the church to buy a chalice and a pyx (a container in which the bread used at communion is placed) and John Hawkyns of "Kynges Houghton" (died 1521) left 6s8d yearly "to the maintenance of the town priest in Houghton."

Bequests were also made for charitable purposes. The Vicar, Wm Walle, left "to the poor of Houghton, Chalgrave and Toddington where most needed £3; 10 poor people in Houghton to be given a gown each."

Road repairs, too were the subject of bequests. Jn. How left 20s "to the repair of Bedwell St., this to be laid in stonys, that ys to say flynts", and Alsone Margery bequeathed "to the reparacion of the hye way towards Cardels, the where moste nede is 12d. Item Y bequeyth to the reparacion of the Chirch Lane callyd the Narrow Lane 12d."

John Hawkyns made several bequests including an acre of land in Sewell Field to his wife Marion. Mrs. Hawkyns was evidently a somewhat formidable lady, for he took care to add "and if she do troble or vex Richard or Robert my sonnys in this my last will in anything to them bequeathed she is to forfeit anything bequeathed to her."

From these wills and the inventories of goods, we can get a good picture of the prosperous yeoman farmers and traders living in and around Houghton at the time of the dissolution of the monasteries.

# CHAPTER 11

## THE DISSOLUTION OF THE MONASTERIES

King Henry VIII had been married to Catherine of Aragon for 18 years, but she had failed to produce a male heir. A legitimate male heir was considered vital to the political stability of the country. Henry charged his Chancellor, Cardinal Thomas Wolsey, Archbishop of York, to obtain the Pope's confirmation that his marriage to Catherine was invalid, since she was his sister in law by her previous marriage. Thomas Wolsey's failure cost him his job.

The "grete and weightie cause" of Henry's divorce was then debated at Dunstable Priory in May 1533, this time with an outcome more satisfactory to the King.

Henry VIII was declared "Supreme Head of the Church of England" by the Act of Supremacy in 1534 and thus split the English church from Rome. In the years which followed, the religious houses of England were completely disbanded. The monasteries had owned about a quarter of the country, and the King as Head of the Church of England laid personal claim to this wealth.

However, locally it seems that the takeover of parish responsibility happened gradually and that the residents were not seriously hurt by the change in land ownership. They had plenty of warning. There was no date on which all religious houses were closed by law; the small monasteries were forced to close or withdraw to motherhouses in 1536, and from then on the larger houses surrendered at various dates up to 1540. In April 1536 there were over 800 religious houses with nearly 10,000 monks, canons, nuns and friars; in April 1540 there were none.

Dunstable Priory surrendered on December 21st 1539. Its Bedfordshire possessions were handled by the Court of Augmentation and rents were paid to accountants and civil servants based at Ampthill.

When the Priory was closed, Henry VIII was the owner of Calcutt (previously the Prior's land) for about a year. The Bray family still owned Eaton and Houghton village. In 1539 Edmund, Lord Bray, died and his wife married Uriah Brereton. She was running Eaton on behalf of her son John, so that when in 1541 Brereton bought Calcutt it was managed by the steward of Eaton Bray and re-united briefly with Houghton village. It then changed hands several times and some time after 1600 was bought by the Medgate family.

The old Calcutt Farm house which was pulled down in 1975 is thought to have been built in the late 16th century (possibly by the Breretons) and not to have been the one built by the Prior.

St Albans Abbey surrendered in 1539, despite the last abbot, Richard Boreman of Stevenage, declaring he would "rather choose to beg his bread all the days of his life than consent to any surrender."

Most of the St. Albans Abbey records were lost, but there is a note that the rectory (greater tithes) and church land were bought by George Cavendish.

George Cavendish appears on the rent list of 1542 as owning several properties in Church Street, including the "Lamme" Inn, "in the right of his wife". It is interesting to note that he was a close companion of Cardinal Wolsey. He is thought to have

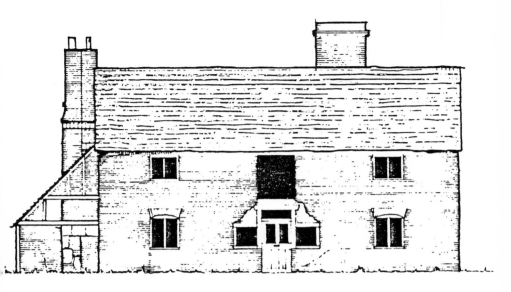

WEST ELEVATION

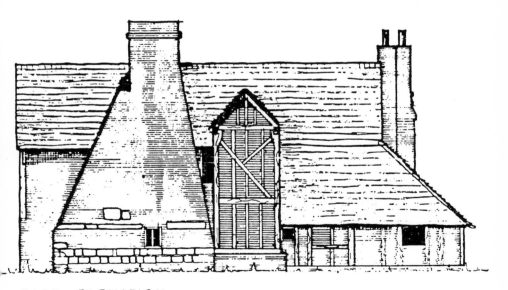

EAST ELEVATION

Fig. 23    The late 16th century Calcutt Farm building pulled
down in 1975. ( J.M.B.)

67

lived at the old royal palace, Kingsbury.

Cavendish died in 1561 having disposed of his estates and the rectory then changed hands several times. What happened to the church lands remains rather obscure, but the advowson or right of presentation of a priest stayed with the crown until Elizabeth I granted (rented) it to Edward Wingate of Harlington. The Wingate family bought a great deal of property in the area which had been owned by the various religious houses and chantries.

In the village itself the name of "Thornbury" was dropped by the end of the 15th century, probably because the two religious houses were less of a threat. The landowners, the Bray Family of Eaton Bray, being resident nearby for at least part of the year, were in complete control. They sold all their estate to Sir Walter Sandys a distant cousin of the Brays in 1574, and the Sandy family held the estate until 1615.

The Dyve family of Sewell seem to have been absentee landlords, although we know that the manor house had its own chapel in use. It may have been used as an estate for a younger son or some relative. In about 1592 it was owned by Sir Lewis Dyve of Bromham.

# CHAPTER 12

## THE DISSOLUTION OF THE CHANTRIES

The Parish Registers at Houghton date from 1538. Up to 1600, the entries are a copy of the original "which was then but in paper....... theise were churchwardens when it was written into parchmente. Thomas Purton and Thomas Wallis in the yeare of our Lord God 1600". From 1600 they were contemporary and are in very good condition.

On the first page of Book 1 is the entry:

"The iij daye of February in the yeare aforesayde (1538) was buried the brotherhood P'ste of Houghton Regis named Richard Whyt."

Richard Whyt was probably acting as chaplain: the living seems to have been vacant for some years until John Couper became Vicar of Houghton and Dunstable in 1554.

Quite apart from the dissolution of the monasteries, great changes took place in the churches themselves during the sixteenth century. Henry VIII wanted to underline the independence of the new national church, and to this end services were to be conducted in English instead of in Latin. Furthermore, each church was to provide two Bibles, one in Latin and one in English for the use of anyone who cared to read them. The great Bible of 1539, the first officially sanctioned Bible in the English

69

Language, was produced under the patronage of Thomas Cromwell, the King's chief adviser. Although Henry had the services conducted in English, however, they were still Catholic in character.

When Henry died in 1547, he was succeeded by Edward VI, nine years old and in poor health. Edward was completely in the hands of his Protector the Duke of Somerset, who was a Protestant.

The use of the new "Book of Common Prayer", more Protestant in tone than the accustomed liturgy, was made law by the Act of Uniformity in Edward's reign.

The government was in deep financial trouble, and chantry chapels in parish churches were richly endowed: the advisers to the young King did not agree with prayer through an intermediary, so they planned to sell the land and houses endowed to support chantries, brotherhoods, lights, Masses and obits for the dead, for the benefit of the crown.

In 1548 Commissioners came to value the chantry property and report on the chaplains. As we already know, John Couper, the chaplain/teacher at Houghton was paid to continue teaching, although all the chantry property was annexed to the crown. The Commissioners scarcely minced their words in their assessment of poor John Couper. They described him as being "xl yeres but menely learned", hardly a glowing recommendation for a schoolmaster!

Also in 1548, the King's Council had further directed that "all things 'corrupt, vain and superstitious'" meaning paintings, statues, the Great Rood, and valuables of all kinds, "should be taken down and destroyed".

All wall paintings would have been whitewashed, the Rood dismantled and everything of value -- gold and silver plate and so on -- was in danger of being annexed to the crown.

The damage to the tomb of John de Sewell may originate from this time, but an expert on church monuments has recently suggested that it is more likely to have been vandalized by local farm labourers using the limbs for sharpening their tools, at this or a later date. Desecrators usually attacked the face of the figure and the prayers sometimes written on small stone tablets issuing from the mouth, but the head is intact in this case, and the limbs are missing.

The Commissioners for Bedfordshire who arrived at Houghton in September 1553 to make an inventory of the church's possessions were L.Sint John, Wryan Brereton, Lewis Dyve and Richard Snow. There was no resident Vicar and so the Churchwardens John Edwardes and Richard Webbe, together with Mathew Pedder, Wylliam Straunge and Thomas Willeys "with other townsmen", "exhybyted" the church's treasures.

The Churchwardens told the Commissioners that there had been a robbery shortly before and thus accounted for the fact that only two plain copes were found, the others having been "stolen when the church was robbed". There is no mention whatever of the figures of saints which figured so prominently in wills of the time. It may well be that the Churchwardens discreetly hid some of the church's more Roman possessions for the occasion. Even so, the inventory lists items used in the Latin Mass:

Three chalices "of the wych one ys silver double gylt waynge xxvij ounces and the other ij be sylver parcell gylt waynge xxvj ounces".

"Item of lattyn ij crosses, too pyxes a payre of sencers a pax and ij lattyn candylstykes".

Ten years later the Bishop heard that the parishioners were using their "superstitious monuments" and ordered that they be removed, so some of the prohibited items evidently survived although we shall never know exactly what they were. The statues of the saints are never directly mentioned again, and what became of these remains a mystery.

The religion of the country veered from one extreme to another, and the local churchwardens and chaplains seem to have managed with commendable diplomacy. When Queen Mary came to the throne in 1553, England once again became Catholic. John Couper was appointed Vicar of both Houghton and Dunstable (meanly learned though he may have been)!

Mary not only took England back to the church of Rome, she consigned some 300 Protestant "heretics" to the flames. Her short and violent reign ended in 1553, and Queen Elizabeth I came to the throne of a kingdom which was religiously divided and nearly bankrupt.

She imposed a religious compromise. Ties with Rome were severed once again by reassertion of the Act of Supremacy; the Book of Common Prayer was re-introduced in a modified form; there was a degree of religious tolerance, but weekly attendance at church was enforced by law, non-attendance bringing a fine of 1s!

John Couper probably accepted the English prayer book. He continued as Vicar and presumably took services at Houghton until he died. In 1563 he was succeeded by George Johnson.

George Johnson was the first of several Vicars presented under the patronage of Elizabeth I, but the incumbents did not necessarily live in the village and may even have held several livings at once; there is evidence that the vicarage was left badly neglected for years.

In the church building itself, we can only guess at the changes which had taken place. Instead of the latin Mass, the Book of Common Prayer was used, services and Bible readings all being in English, giving ordinary people an access to the liturgy which had previously been unknown.

Much of the colour, drama and ornamentation was gone: we know that the painted and gilded saints' figures were missing, and the rich chantry and fraternity chapels. The walls were probably whitewashed as opposed to painted with texts between the bays of the nave; the Rood would probably have been replaced by the Royal Coat of Arms.

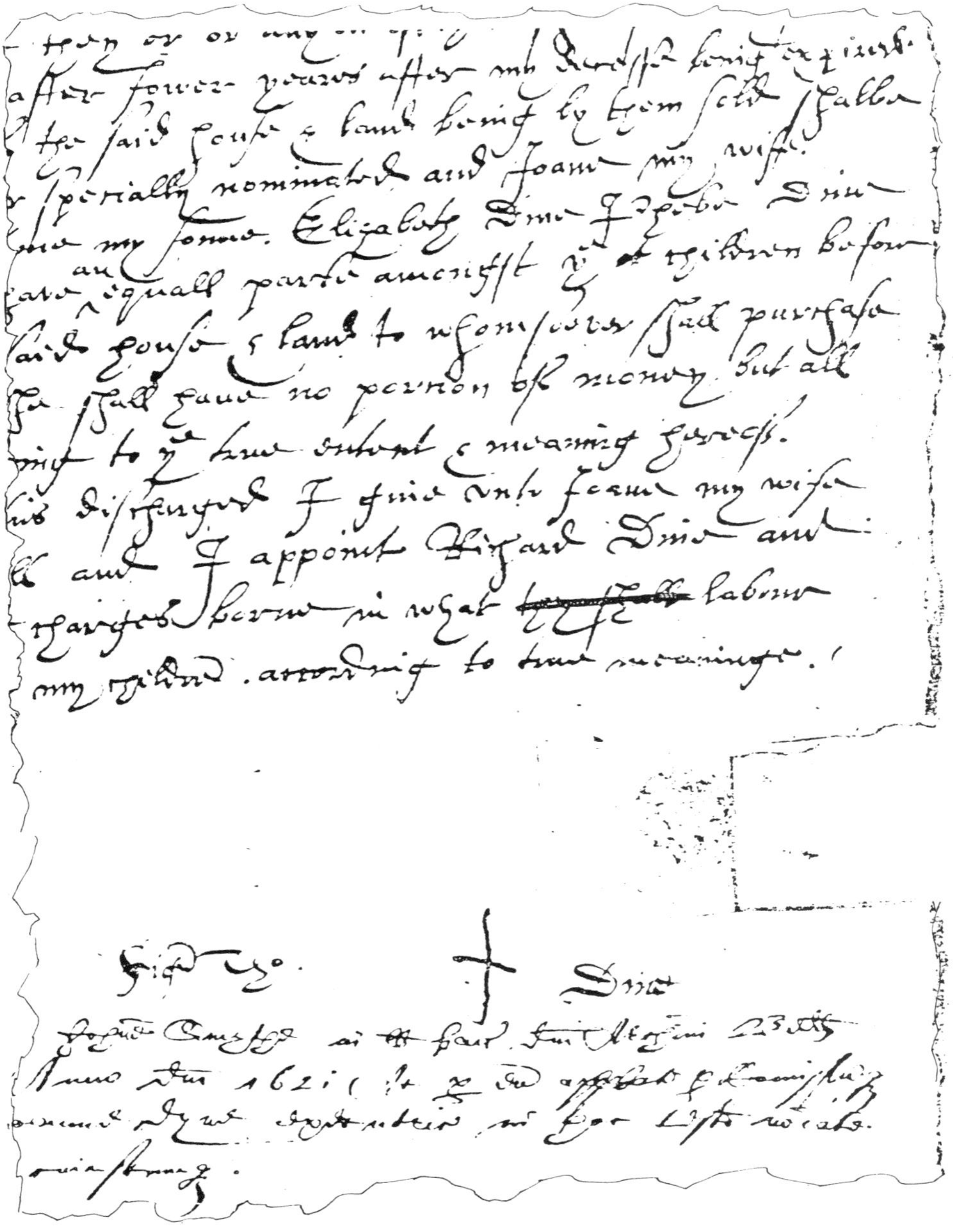

Fig. 24  Part of the will of Thomas Dyne of Bidwell (1621). (C.R.O.)

# CHAPTER 13

## THE BRANDRETHS

The 1542 rent list for Dunstable showed a subtle
shift in the character of the town, away from an
economy based on catering for the needs of wealthy
businessmen and merchants towards that of an
agricultural market town with a growing tourist
industry of travellers' inns and beerhouses. Either
economy provided a sound market for Houghton farmers
and artisans who continued to prosper into the 17th
Century.

A contemporary will shows Thomas Dyne of Bidwell,
Houghton Regis in 1621 (described as a labourer)
making careful provision of his two acres of arable
land in "Caldicott", two half-acres in the Northfield,
a furlong behind Bidwell, his house with another acre
adjoining, and all his possessions. The unfortunate
Mrs Dyne is required to "yield up" the house when it
is sold four years after the death of her husband "and
if she refuseth so to do contrary to this decree then
she shall have no portion of money but all the money
shall be divided between the children"! Apparently
another redoubtable Houghton lady, needing to be
firmly handled even from the hereafter!

During the 17th century, much of Houghton was
gradually brought together under the ownership of the
Brandreth family, who were then and until early this
century a major influence in the village. Their first

acquisition was Sewell, which from about 1592 had been owned by Sir Lewis Dyve, of Bromham.

During this period Charles I was at loggerheads with Parliament, and in the end both sides raised armies and the country found itself engaged in Civil War.

Locally, the landowners tended to support the King, but the people were "for Parliament". Sir Lewis Dyve became a senior officer in the Royalist army and consequently his estates were sequestrated by Parliament.

Because Bedfordshire was controlled by the Parliamentary army, the residents had to supply a proportion of everything required for their camp at Newport Pagnell. Not only were soldiers impressed, but also labourers, horses, carts, tools, materials and food. Careful accounts were kept but payment was slow and resources could not be spared. In addition, the Royalists sent out raiding parties from their headquarters at Oxford and these frequent forays for men, horses and food brought farming to a standstill and, locally, caused great hardship.

Eventually the Royalists were defeated. Charles I was beheaded and in 1649 England became a Commonwealth under Oliver Cromwell, whose civil servants began to sell the sequestered estates.

By September 1652, Henry Brandreth had bought Sewell from the sequestrators; he was a wealthy businessman who, like many others, at this time chose to buy a country estate. He may have brought in a relative, Joseph, to look after his investment at Sewell, as there is a record of a "Joseph Brandreth, of Kings Houghton, gentleman", accused of battery at the Bedford Sessions of 1657. This was settled out of court; it may have been a comparatively minor affair and have had political connotations. However, after the Restoration of Charles II the Dyve family regained their sequestered estates, including Sewell, but Henry Brandreth came to a financial arrangement with them and kept Sewell, which was let to a local farmer.

In c1653, Henry was able to buy the advowson at Houghton, but at that time the rectory had been sold separately so the Brandreth family could not acquire it until 1691.

The manor of Houghton had been held by the Sandys' family until 1615, when it was sold to a barrister of the Middle Temple who in turn passed it to John Egerton, first Earl of Bridgewater. It was managed as part of the Ashridge Estate until John Egerton's son sold it to Henry Brandreth somewhere about 1654 (exact date unknown) and the Brandreths then became Lords of the Manor of Houghton Regis.

It seems likely that Henry Brandreth, who was a wealthy businessman, continued for some years living in London. He was a member of the Clothworkers Guild and well respected in the City; his name appears as a proposer on the nominations of Aldermen of the City of London (in 1670 a Henry Brandreth was nominated, but not accepted). In 1656 he was a commissioner for "securing peace in the city of London", and from time to time was appointed to various investigative committees.

Henry seems to have been particularly adroit at treading the political minefields of his time. His personal fortunes flourished during the time of the Commonwealth when he provided supplies for the Navy, and when the Monarchy was restored, he was sufficiently well regarded by Charles II for him to intervene personally on Henry's behalf, to protect his reputation. Charles wrote to the Lord Mayor of London: "having received good satisfaction concerning the peaceable disposition and loyalty of Henry Brandreth and understanding that certain persons for private revenges have threatened to discredit and disgrace him... ye may not act anything to his prejudice before you have communicated to one of our Principal Secretaries of State, being very unwilling if anyone should use your authority as the instrument of their private malice and vex or disquiet our good subject under the specious disguise of loyalty". (State Papers Domestic 24th October 1662).

Two years later in 1664, when War with Holland was imminent, Henry was "examined before Lord Arlington" as to his relationship with the Dutch Ambassador. He replied that he didn't even know where the Dutch Ambassador lived! "Being further asked whether hee hath not been lately in company with any discontented or seditious persons about the town answers confidently that he hath at no time met any of them except he met them by chance as other people in the street and asked how they did or so". (State Papers Domestic 12th June 1665).

Henry may have had his enemies like most wealthy businessmen, but he was also capable of being a very good friend. George Villiers (a relative of the Duke of Buckingham) wrote to him gratefully, for having transferred money to help Villiers' son "in a forregne land".

Fig. 25
The Brandreth coat of arms. (G.M.N.)

In 1652 when Henry Brandreth first bought land in Houghton Regis, he was 42 years old and married to Alice Hawford; they had a ten year old son named

Solomon and a three year old daughter named Alice. During the year a second son was baptised at St Stephens Wallbrook. His name was Nehemiah.

Unfortunately, Solomon, Henry's eldest son, appears to have been retarded in some way and special provision had always to be made for him. His behaviour caused the family some anxiety, as the years went on.

The manor house at Houghton was evidently large and comfortable: we know from the hearth tax that twelve of the rooms were provided with a fireplace and from a later inventory that they had log baskets. There was plenty of wood to be had from the estate and at a later date 'sea coal' was available at Bulbourne Wharf, near Tring. In her will, Henry's wife Alice mentions the extensive accommodation for the servants. Having bequeathed her jewellery to her daughter Alice, she ordered that all her linen and drapery should be divided by "indifferent appraisers" between her three children, but Nehemiah, who was going to be responsible for running the house, received in addition

- The brewhouse with all its equipment
- The household goods and implements belonging to the kitchen
- The (servants?) hall next to the kitchen
- The parlour next to the hall (butler and/or housekeepers room?)
- The bedsteads and bedding in the men's chamber over the (servants') parlour
- The bed and bedding 'where the maid usually lyeth'.

So the family settled down at the 'big house' right in the centre of the village, where Henry took his responsibilities as country landowner very seriously.

As she grew up, the question of his daughter

Alice's marriage had to be considered; as a businessman, Henry was aware of the risks in choosing a husband for a young girl whose father's wealth sprang from the city. The surviving correspondence shows that he used a variety of excuses to refuse what he considered to be unsuitable offers. Alice was obviously the apple of her father's eye and no one was 'truly virtuous' enough.

When all these negotiations fell through, he assured her independence by giving her an estate at Ware in Hertfordshire. In the meantime, she continued to live with the family at Houghton.

On March 2nd 1673, Henry Brandreth died. In his will he carefully provided for his family. His wife Alice was to continue living in the family house, and to oversee the running of the estate since Nehemiah was only twenty-one.£3,000 was set aside as a marriage portion for daughter Alice and she was to be one of the trustees whom he appointed to watch over his provisions for the 31 year old Solomon. Henry knew that Solomon could not manage his own money, but he wanted to be sure that he could continue to live in comfort. Not only did Solomon receive an annuity in trust, but also an honest and discreet servant to 'look to him the said Solomon.'

After her father's death, Alice moved out of the family home and went to live on her estate at Ware, and some years later she married Thomas Smyth of Binderston in Sussex. Solomon died in the same year, and so Alice received a further income of £45 p.a. from the rectory land at Houghton which had provided part of Solomon's annuity. Before she married, she invested part of her inheritance in a small estate in Stanbridge (between Houghton and Leighton Buzzard) called "Raynes" or "Morteynes".

Henry Brandreth's wife died in March 1683. Nehemiah, the second son, had stayed on in Houghton

Fig. 26
Rebecca Price's coat of arms.

with his mother, and by the time of her death he had
already met and was planning to marry Rebecca Price
from Westbury in Buckinghamshire. Rebecca was 23
years old and a very suitable match. She was well
qualified to run a large estate, and her family
background was very similar to that of the Brandreths.

Her grandfather, who had made a fortune in the
city, had bought Westbury manor from the widow of an
ardent royalist. They had a coat of arms which
included 'three cloughs' (wingless birds) which many
years later would be incorporated into the Brandreth
coat of arms.

When Rebecca was in her teens, she was sent to a
boarding school at Hackney where she learnt cookery
and household management. It was a sort of 'finishing
school' for young ladies likely to have to manage a
large household. It was while she was there that she
began to collect recipes, including some that had been
used by her mother. When she left school she may have
travelled abroad with her father, because some of her
recipes are "given me at Montpelier in France" and she
also had a "french receipt: given me by Monsieur le
Marqui Achioler" for "Melindes" which seem to be
meringues.

Because Rebecca's family had a house in St Paul's
Churchyard, Rebecca and Nehemiah were married on 1st
October 1683 at St Paul's Church in Covent Garden.

Rebecca moved in to the manor house at Houghton where she seems to have made many friends in the neighbourhood. She continued collecting recipes and entered them into a calfbound folio. It includes recipes given her by her sister, Anne, (Kersteman, buried at All Saints Church), other family and friends including "Mrs Dunscombe" (possibly from the Bedfordshire Dunscombes, as her granddaughter married Wm Dunscombe of Chalgrave), "Mrs Beech" from Redbourne (her younger daughter married Thomas Beech), Lady Napier (possibly of Luton Hoo) and Mrs Whitehead. She also included some of the recipes which were used by the cooks at Westbury and Houghton.

It is interesting to note that in her will Rebecca mentions two books — her collection of recipes, and a book of other notes on household management. The recipe book was found several years ago and published in a modern edition by Madeleine Masson.

Nehemiah (1) lived to be 67, and Rebecca saw her eightieth birthday. Their eldest son, Henry (2) married Mary Chibbald from Kent, and they had four children, three girls and a boy Henry (3).

The third Henry was only 16 years old when in 1739 he inherited the main family estate: six years later, he married his cousin Rebecca Beech from Redbourn.

The young Henry was not in the best of health, and did not expect to have children of his own, but on the other hand, he had three sisters for whom he had to provide marriage portions, and a large house which was probably in need of a great deal of repair. Two years before he died, although he was only 26, he sold the family home and estate to the Duke of Bedford. The Brandreth family ceased to be major property owners in the village.

However, the Brandreth connection with Houghton was kept up by the original Brandreth's daughter Alice(1).

Fig. 27   One of the Brandreth estate cottages, still standing in Drury Lane. In this photograph, the tenant (on the right) is Charlotte Hudson, a laundress.   (T.C.)

By 1692 her husband Thomas Smyth had died and Alice was living alone on the estate at Ware. She was an extremely wealthy widow; in addition to her inheritance from both her father and then her husband, her mother had bequeathed her a "necklace of oriental pearls, a jewel of diamonds, one great silver flagon, one silver chaffing dish with one great silver bason".

She was widowed at the age of only 43, and having no children of her own decided to move back to Houghton to be near her brother Nehemiah, his wife Rebecca and their children the 7 year old Henry (2) 4 year old Nehemiah (2) and 6 year old daughter Alice (2).

In March of the same year she bought for £6,000 the remaining rectory land and the greater tithes and in May she paid £1,750 for yet another large piece of land, on the Luton side of the village.

By the end of the year she had remarried. Before the wedding, she prudently put into trust (where no husband could get at them) all those family and personal possessions which she might be expected to pass to the Brandreth nephews and nieces. It is possible that this was a love match which caused her family some concern.

Her new husband was William Milard of London, who was soon to be knighted, making her Dame Alice Milard. In 1695, William was made High Sheriff of Bedfordshire, a post which had been held in 1671 by Alice's father, Henry.

Alice and William Milard had a great mansion house built on the land she had bought on the opposite side of the village green to the old manor house. This was the present Houghton Hall. It was finished in 1700 and she lived there with her husband until his death on New Year's Day 1710.

Fig. 28   Houghton Hall as it appears today. (O.R.)

There is a monument to commemorate Alice's parents and brothers and Sir Wm Milard in the Chancel of All Saints Church. It was ordered by Alice and erected 18 months after her death.

Alice lived at Houghton Hall for another 19 years after the death of her second husband, and by that time both her parents and her two brothers had died. Her 70 year old sister-in-law Rebecca was living across the Green at the old manor house with her son Henry (2) daughter-in-law Mary and their three children. This family would inherit the main estates and were well provided for, so Alice (1) left her mansion house to her younger nephew Nehemiah (2) having already made provisions for her nieces who shared between them their grandmother's jewellery.

By the time he inherited Houghton Hall from his Aunt Alice, Nehemiah (2) was a widower with three teenage children.

It is likely that Isabella, the youngest (named after her mother) lived with her grandmother, Rebecca. Isabella did not marry until she was 34. Her husband Thomas Baskerfield of Redbourn, lived to a ripe old age of 80; Isabella died four months later.

We don't know exactly what happened to the old manor house thereafter. It was at least 100 years old. The old "coach house" is marked on 19th century maps standing out in the road near today's Drury Lane, but there is no trace of the manor house.

The second son, Nehemiah (3) became an attorney and handled the family's legal affairs. In 1753 he married Frances Alston who was an heiress of the Alston Family of Odell. They lived first in Toddington and then at Dunstable, but at the age of only 40, Nehemiah died. He was buried in Houghton Regis church; his monument records that his "wife and five children were left unconsolable".

86

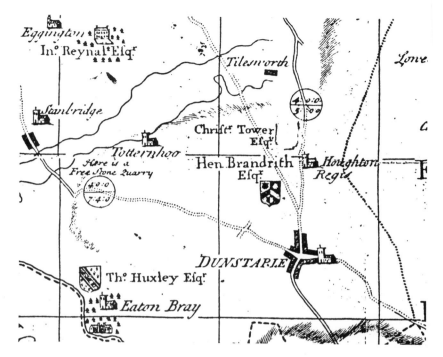

Fig. 29     Part of "an accurate map of the County of Bedford"
(Wm. Gordon Grant 1736) showing the Brandreth coat
of arms.

It was the eldest son Thoswithan who inherited the
mansion house and estates from his father.  He had
studied to be a 'Doctor of Physicke' at Oxford, and
had degrees in both Arts and Medicine.

Thoswithan seems to be a portmanteau name; it is
probably a combination of Thomas William and Henry –
all family names.  Thoswithan lived only six years
after his father's death, but during that time he got
into serious financial difficulties.  He had no
understanding of money.  A surviving document written
by a creditor after his death records "Thoswithan
Brandreth deceased proved a very improvident man and
brought himself to the necessity of borrowing money
continually".

His widow Mary, nee Buckeridge returned to her family in London, taking with her their two young daughters and 12 year old Thoswithan (2).

Thoswithan (2) inherited his father's estate, but he had no Brandreth uncles to help and advise him and the inheritance soon fell into a worse state than ever. Much of it was mortgaged. His own mother had to take him to law to make him pay her the annuity that her late husband - his father - had left her.

At the age of 17 Thoswithan (2) entered Lincoln's Inn where he spent his time enjoying himself. While he was living in London he married and had several children. He moved back to Houghton where he died aged 48, leaving his debts and heavily mortgaged estate to his only son, Henry (4).

Henry was 17 when he inherited, and was totally different in character from his father and grandfather. He set about managing his estates efficiently and reviving the family fortunes.

He married his cousin Dionisia Turner, when he was 22. This must have been a love match, since Dionisia was a wealthy heiress and could presumably have married very well indeed. Instead she chose Henry, and it certainly wasn't to increase her fortune. Arrangements were made before the marriage for her property in Devon and Cornwall to be sold; this money put the Houghton estates in order once more.

The Brandreths again played their traditional role in the community; Henry became Justice of the Peace, High Sheriff of Bedfordshire, Trustee of Dunstable Charity School and an ubiquitous member of local committees.

Henry and Dionisia had one child, Henry (5). Sadly Henry (5) died, before his father, at the age of 40 and without having married. Henry (4) then was left with no son of his own to inherit Houghton Hall and his estates.    He chose as his heir the son of his youngest sister, Sarah Prosser.    Sarah had married into the Gibbs family of Ampthill.    The Gibbs were very respected: Thomas, Sarah's husband, was seedsman to the Board of Agriculture.    He did research into the growing of cereal crops and was appointed Honorary Secretary of the Royal Agricultural Society and also ran the family business of seed merchants with branches at Ampthill and Picadilly.

Sarah and Thomas' son Humphrey Gibbs inherited Houghton Hall and the Brandreth lands when he was 39.

> There were several conditions of his inheritance,
>
> . he was to change his name to Brandreth
> . he was to adopt the Brandreth coat of arms
> . he was to live in Houghton Hall for at least three months of the year
> . the terms of the will regarding the estate could not be altered in any way.

Humphrey set to work to fulfil the conditions of his inheritance.    On October 27th 1846, the announcement of his change of name appeared in the London Gazette: "The Queen has been pleased to grant unto Humphrey Gibbs of Houghton House in the parish of Houghton Regis, in the county of Bedford, Esq. eldest surviving son of Thomas Gibbs of Ampthill in the said county of Bedford and of Old Brompton, in the county of Middlesex by Sarah Prosser, his wife, and at length sole heir of Henry Brandreth late of Houghton House aforesaid, Esq. deceased, Her royal licence and authority that, in compliance with a proviso contained in the last will of his maternal uncle, the said Henry Brandreth, he may take and use the surname of Brandreth, instead of his present surname of Gibbs,

and the arms of Brandreth quarterly in the first
quarter with his own family arms, and that such
surname and arms may be taken and born by his
issue....".

Fig. 30
The arms of Humphrey Gibbs
Brandreth.

It cost Humphrey £120 to change his name and to
register his new arms. He wanted the most magnificent
coat of arms possible, and on 29th October 1846,
received a letter from the College of Arms assuring
him as to the grandness and fidelity of the
representation of the Arms and not least as to the
etiquette involved in Her Majesty's granting of them.
"With respect to the Arms," writes William
Cleethorpes, Rouge Croix, "the painting I sent you was
but a rough affair and wherever yellow was there used
it will be Gold in the Patent-the usual bearings in
Heraldry are so contrary to nature that our painters
(in depicting objects) are wont to forget nature and
heraldic shadowing has become as unlike real light
and shade, as heraldic lions are unlike real lions,
nevertheless in the points you mention we will strive
as nearly as possible to meet your wishes consistent
with heraldic usage. The pommel and hilt of the Sword
will be proper in the Patent which in Heraldic usage
is Gold. The Mullet is also gold and I will direct
the Painter to shade it with not so red a colour but
one more adapted to the metals. There will be no

necessity to show the inside of the Gauntlet at all or very little of it and it shall be all steel without the gold garniture (as we call the rims and edges of armour) - the hands in the Arms of Gibbs shall be gauntletted in like fashion.

"Pray do not consider it necessary to make any apology for your remarks, I am only too glad to be able to make such slight alterations as you have very properly suggested".

He concludes, "Etiquette does not require you to take any notice of the Grant from Her Majesty".

Humphrey was only too willing to take the name and arms of the Brandreths, but when it came to the proviso of actually living at Houghton Hall, he was not too keen. The house was now nearly 150 years old, and in his lawyer's words "incommodious and delapidated". He wanted to pull the old house down and build a new mansion, but the terms of the will were very specific. Humphrey took Counsel's opinion. The answer was an emphatic "No"; he could not pull the house down. So Humphrey had the house renovated, at his own expense, by Henry Clutton, architect, and Samual Grimsdell, builder. It cost him £4,508, but saved for posterity the building which still stands on the Green.

Humphrey did come to live at the Hall, and in his turn took on the role of country squire. He was a Justice of the Peace, became High Sheriff of Bedfordshire in 1849, and concerned himself closely with the organisation of All Saints Church. He served on many local committees and was trustee of local schools. He extended the Houghton estates and made them more efficient and profitable.

He married at the age of 47. His bride was Emma Smith, heiress of Lt. Col Harvey Smith of Aspley

Fig. 31
Henry Chernocke Gibbs Brandreth.

House. Humphrey and Emma had two children, Alice and
Henry Chernocke Gibbs Brandreth.

When Humphrey Gibbs Brandreth died in 1864, his son
and heir Henry Chernocke Gibbs Brandreth was aged only
eight. Henry's mother, Emma Smith, died when he was
eleven, but fortunately his uncles on the Gibbs family
side were able to guide the young boy, especially his
Aunt Rebecca's husband John Brodribb Bergne.

Henry was educated at Rugby, and matriculated from
St Johns College Oxford in 1875. In 1879 he married
Evelyn Lawton from Cheshire.

Like the Brandreths before him, Henry was a Justice
of the Peace, High Sheriff of Bedfordshire; trustee of
Dunstable Charity School and of Houghton Free School,
and on numerous local committees. He was also the
first elected representative of Houghton Regis on the
County Council and, since the manor lands had been
re-acquired by the Brandreth estate, Lord of the Manor
of Houghton Regis. He took an active interest in the
running of the Thomas Whitehead (Free) school,
inspecting it regularly, and signing the log-book. He

was Patron of the living of Houghton Regis, and in 1883 presented William Faux Lovell as Vicar. The Reverend Lovell died at an early age, having been Vicar for only just over five years and was later commemorated by carved panels representing the four Evangalists added to the present stone pulpit. In 1889 Henry presented William Wedge to the living.

Henry was noted for his interest in the Houghton Regis Fire Brigade. He was founder, patron and honorary Captain. He built a new Fire Station just in front of the Church and presented the Brigade with a new engine, hoses and equipment. The Brigade took part in friendly competitions with neighbouring Fire Brigades, and nothing delighted the Squire more than to be on the Fire Engine with his men.

When he died, the Dunstable Gazette of January 29th 1908 records, "It was no cause for wonder, therefore, that the interment should take the character of a Fireman's Funeral nor that the members of the neighbouring brigades should muster in full strength to pay the last respect to the departed Honorary Captain....."

"The procession, which presented a most impressive spectacle as it slowly crossed the Green, was led by Superintendent Panter and Inspector Mason with a detachment of Beds County Police. Next came members of the various Fire Brigades proceeding and alongside of the Houghton Regis Fire Engine which was drawn by four beautiful Flemish horses: the engine had been chastely decorated with white flowers and wreathes and on it was borne the polished and massively furnished oak coffin containing the remains of the deceased. On the coffin were other magnificent wreaths."

The Gazette recalled happier days:

"There are those still living in the village who

Fig. 32    An early fire pump photographed by the park wall of Houghton Hall.    (C.R.O.)

can remember the rejoicings at the birth of the late Squire and many more who can recall the festivities at his coming of age 30 years ago when a bullock was roasted on the village green".

The funeral was a huge affair, reported in every detail in the local press. It was the end of an era.

Henry and Evelyn had had three children, Frances, Barbara and William, but none of them inherited Houghton Hall. When Henry died his estates were sold off - they covered most of Houghton Regis stretching from Blows Downs to Lords Hill and across to Dunstable. Houghton Hall was sold to Colonel Parts.

The elder son Frances went to South Africa; all of Frances' children had died before 1984. Barbara did not marry and died in 1941. The youngest son William married; his wife's mame was Gertrude Maude and their son the Reverend Henry (7) Renault Turner Brandreth was the last in the line of the family.

The Reverend Henry had a very distinguished career: he was educated in Devon and then Sheffield University. He went on to Lincoln Theological College and was ordained deacon in 1942, and priest in 1943.

Henry was appointed Curate of Paris in 1949. He was a well respected theological author and an authority on East European religions. On his return to London in 1965, he was closely connected with St Dunstans, Fleet Street, where a memorial service was held when he died in 1984. The service was attend by the Vicar and parishioners from Houghton, and his death was marked in Houghton Regis by the tolling of the bell at All Saints, exactly as the passing of so many Brandreths had been marked over the centuries. His ashes were interred in the family vault at the east end of the church, the last of the Brandreth line.

Fig. 33    The Houghton Regis Fire Brigade in front of the Fire Station. (A.J.)

Here lyeth y̆ body of Solomon Brandreth gen eldest sonn of Henry Brandreth esq̃ and Alice [his] wife) who dyed in th 4...

Here lyeth y̆ body of M[rs] Alice [the] widdow of Henry Brandreth es died in y̆ Lord abovt y̆ 70th yeare of H age on y̆ 2[:] day of March 168...

Here doth a vertvovs & gracious wo... Whilst Christ y̆ Lord of Life calls her him fo... Then over blest no dovbt when raised ... At the Great Jvdgment day from...

Fig. 34    Memorial marbles to the Brandreth family in the chancel of All Saints Church. (O.R.)

All over the chancel at All Saints are memorial marbles to the Brandreth family who were buried in the family vault under the sanctuary. This vault has been sealed for over a hundred years, and been replaced by a brick vault outside the east wall.

There is a chair in the sanctuary presented by Henry Chernocke Gibbs Brandreth. Over the north door of the chancel is a hatchment bearing the arms of Humphrey Gibbs Brandreth, and an even older Brandreth hatchment hangs on the opposite wall. (Hatchments were square panels set cornerwise bearing the coat of arms of a deceased person and hung outside the house, then often later hung in church, as these are).

The ends of the choir stalls have various heraldic items from the Brandreth achievements carved on them - shells, a gauntletted hand, etc: the choir stalls were put in in 1913.

Fig. 35 The Brandreth achievements carved on the choir stalls in
All Saints Church.

# CHAPTER 14

## THE FREE SCHOOL

The death of John Couper, the Houghton teacher/curate in c1555 was significant in ways which could never have been apparent at the time.

His death marked the beginning of a long period of neglect for the Houghton vicarage.  On May 29th 1656 a petition was put before Oliver Cromwell, drawing his attention to the "Parish of Houghton Regis County Bedford consisting of four villages (i.e. Thorn, Sewell, Calcutt and Houghton village itself) and many hundred souls who have not had a preaching minister these hundred years because the vicarage is only small tithes of £20 a year to be collected from 200 persons and hardly paying the labour of collecting".

Subsequently, Parliament awarded Houghton £55 per annum to help attract an incumbent.  Henry Brandreth bought the advowson in 1653, but it was not until August 1661, after the restoration of Charles II that he succeeded in appointing a resident vicar, the Rev. James Paddon.

The reference to Houghton not having a preaching minister "these hundred years" may have been approximate, but it was essentially true.  The Rev. Roger Rogers lived in the village from 1588-1605, but was not a graduate, nor was he qualified to preach.

The status of the Rev. Thomas Tomkins B.A. who was presented in 1607 is rather uncertain. He was certainly resident, but may well not have preached, or he may have held several other livings. He married six weeks after his presentation, settled in the village, and had a family. It was he who prepared a terrier (inventory) of the old vicarage building from which we know that it was a two-storeyed building with one main downstairs room a "chicken (!kitchen) buttery and backhouse and two other necessary rooms".

What is sure, however, is that for a very long period prior to the presentation of the petition to Cromwell, Houghton's services were taken by a panel of "lecturers" serving the area. There was no resident Vicar under this scheme and the whole arrangement was unsatisfactory and unpopular.

The death of John Couper also meant that the Dyve school closed, leaving Houghton seriously lacking in educational facilities. The Priory had had a school, but it had itself been closed down during the reign of Henry VIII, and there was no local resident priest to do a little part-time teaching in the traditional way.

Rich men could send their sons away to be educated, of course. When they were 18-19 years old, if they had got a basic education in reading, writing, arithmetic and religious study, they could matriculate at a university (rather like taking A levels).

The growing demand for commercial accommodation for both men and horses, which followed the closing of the Priory, bought prosperity to both business men and farmers at Houghton, as a result of which they would have liked to educate their sons even though they could not afford to send them away to school, so the lack of educational facilities must have been a cause for local concern.

One family which prospered at this period was the Whiteheads; they had a house on the green called "Stranges". Thomas Whitehead claims in his will to have been born there, but no baptismal entry can be traced for him.

He is probably the Thomas who studied for Matric at Magdelene College, 1635, and studied for his degree between 1638-1639.

A 'relative' (probably his father) had been headmaster at Repton School, Derbyshire, where Thomas became First Usher (senior master) from 1642 until he died in 1654.

At the age of only 43, Thomas became seriously ill. He returned to Houghton Regis, but by the time he made his will, he was so weak he could only scratch his mark; however, he was perfectly clear in his mind as to what he wanted to do with the family property.

'Stranges', the house which Thomas Whitehead had inherited, faced the village Green; it had various outbuildings and 1/4 acre of land. He instructed that either it should be converted into a school house and classroom or be pulled down and the materials used to build a new, specially designed school.

The first two schoolmasters were local vicars who did not need a school house and it is likely that the first group of boys were taught in the church while a new building was being erected. Later documents describe a school house and school room which suggests that the premises were purpose built.

In addition to the house and garden, Thomas Whitehead left the large sum of £250, and when the expenses of setting-up the school were complete, the remainder was invested in 15 acres in England's Field (the 'inlands' behind Station Rd) Dunstable.

An Abstract from the Will of Thomas Whitehead dated

Proprietor of the Lordshews of Repton (or Repindon) in the County of Derby bearing date the tenth day of September in the year 1654. Among others is as followeth.

Whereas I stand seized of an Estate of Inheritance ... and in and ... forcage farm or Tenement with the Thirdman ... it called the Thorps being the place of my Birth to which ... my great respect ... Houghton-Regis in the County of Bedford. I give and bequeath the same to my Executors hereafter named and their Heirs for ever together with Two Hundred and Forty pounds of lawful English money to the intent and purpose that any such Executors shall with what convenient speed they can after my decease convert part of my ... dwelling house or Building thereunto belonging into a School House

102

In his will, Thomas Whitehead had stipulated that the school should be made up of 15 boys from poor families in Houghton and five boys from poor families in the hamlets (probably Thorn, Calcutt and Sewell). But some of his instructions were confused e.g. 'pay unto some honest and painful (painstaking) schoolmaster who shall be employed to keep school and teach twenty scholars freely without any salary for his pains....' This statement could be interpreted in various ways: but probably meant that no fees should be charged and, as it became by custom, no salary as such should be paid, the master having the right to let the 15 acres, take the entire income and be responsible for the upkeep of the school.

The executors and their heirs were to be responsible for choosing both masters and boys and for watching over the maintenance of the buildings, in return for which he left them the rest of his earthly goods.

He obviously realised that "their heirs" was too vague a phrase for such responsibility, so he ended his will by saying that if they "think meet", they should "settle and convey the said lands upon six of the most substantial inhabitants in Houghton....as learned counsel shall advise".

In 1654, Henry Brandreth was just establishing himself as lord of the manor. One of the three witnesses to Thomas Whitehead's will was Roger Brandreth, who may have been a relative of Henry's.

The will was dictated in 1654, during the Protectorate, when it was not popular to favour the Church of England, so he did not suggest that a representative from the church should be an executor, nor did he stipulate that the children should be from church going families.

Houghton was one of the villages whose vicarage had been sequestered by Parliament, and as their services were taken by a team of lecturers, it was the vicar of Totternhoe, the Reverend Daniel Clethro who became first headmaster; he was approaching 70 years old and held the position for less than two years.

What sort of experience school proved to be for the children involved is a matter for conjecture, but quite apart from the Rev. Clethro's advanced age, he would have taught from such books as he had for his own use - collected sermons perhaps, "improving" texts and at the most horn books, slates and the like. There would not have been the attractive and child oriented textbooks we associate with school today.

The Rev. Clethro died in 1657, and the Rev. James Paddon arrived in Houghton having been appointed by Henry Brandreth. He was a much younger man and lived in the vicarage for the next 45 years or so. He and his wife arrived with two young sons and soon had a family of eight. He must have had an assistant living in the school house; in 1671 both the school and the vicarage were tax assessed for 3 hearths. It is probable that when he was old enough, James' son Francis moved into the school house, because when his father died in 1704, Francis at 36 years old, became the next master.

We know very little about the daily routine of the school during the first 150 years except that it was only open to boys and that there was no religious bias in either teaching or selection.

From later events we can assume that the school day was 9.00 am to 12.00 noon and 2.00 pm to 5.00 pm in summer, 4.00 pm in winter, six days a week. The main subjects taught were: reading, writing, spelling and arithmetic, but over the years as the church gained influence, the teaching of the catechism was included.

When Francis Paddon was buried in 1731 he was described as 'late schoolmaster'. Information about his succesor has not survived. The next recorded master is John Lesley, who arrived at the school house in 1773. These was no retirement age specified and each of the first four recorded resident masters held the job for at least 25 years!

There is no reference to Francis Paddon having a second job for his support when he was schoolmaster, but he appears to have been a bachelor with no wife and family to keep. John Lesley who probably found the school house in need of repair and the garden neglected when he took over, certainly had the expense of a large growing family.

The pasture land in Dunstable was not bringing in sufficient for his needs, so he improved the garden, and with the help of his sons (and probably his pupils) planted vegetables and soft fruit bushes. To make the school more profitable, he arranged to take private paying pupils, in addition to the charity boys, and made both groups bring their own pens, ink and firing. Also in an attempt to bring in even more money, he applied for all the part-time clerical jobs that became vacant in the area.

In addition to his duties as schoolmaster, Mr Lesley became an officer in the Bedfordshire Yeomanry and took part in manoeuvres on Dunstable Downs, near the old "Rifle Volunteer". He also held other jobs, such as clerk to the Justices of the Peace. His additional clerical jobs required office and storage space, and by demolishing the big central chimney piece and replacing the large open fire in the classroom, he was able to construct a tiny office.

Somehow, he found the money to buy for his classroom a metal stove which had its own metal chimney. This meant that the children, who had been

West Parade, Dunstaple.

Fig. 37    The old "Rifle Volunteer" by the Downs.    (L.F.)

bringing fallen branches for the open fire, had to bring expensive coal.

Furthermore, as Mr Lesley spent more time on his county work and his own children were increasingly called in to do the teaching, there were complaints from the village. During the time that he was schoolmaster, there are more references to his work as Captain of the Yeomanry, Secretary to the Justices of the Peace and Secretary to the Lord Lt of the County, than there are to his success or otherwise as a schoolmaster, although it transpires later that the parents were complaining about his neglect of the children as early as 1805.

The complaints were compounded by the fact that Mr Lesley who was a churchwarden at All Saints included the catechism in his lessons. This was bound to cause friction in a village with a Methodist Chapel at Thorn, a Baptist Chapel in the High Street, and a Quaker Meeting House at Sewell.

When he made his will, Thomas Whitehead could never have forseen the difficulties that would overtake the school in the distant future.

1.  Because of the political/religious difficulties of the time, he could not make it a "church" school and put it under the control of a local vicar or rector. It therefore had no one in the village directly responsible for its organisation.

2.  He did not foresee that when the building began to need a lot of repairs, there would be a problem about dividing the income of his endowment between salary and repairs.

3.  He could not forsee the agricultural depression which would mean that the value of his land would fall.

4.  Nor could he foresee that of the original three executors the "Rev. Roger Jacson, George and Roger Allestry, Gentlemen and their heirs", by 1800 the Allestry family would be extinct and 100% control of the school would be in the hands of an elderly man living in Cheshire, the Rev. Simon Jacson.

As the years went by and his family became more numerous, Mr Lesley became worried about the future. His older sons showed no interest in teaching, and the family were living in a 'tied' cottage.

The first suggestion that things might go wrong, is in a letter that John Lesley wrote in 1808. Word had got round that the Rev. Jacson wanted to give up the responsibility of being sole remaining executor, so John Lesley wrote to ask if Mr Jacson would let him "obtain the patronage" of the school. He pointed out that he had "numerous family", that the rent from the endowment land was only £30 per annum and that the constant repairs meant that the house could not be considered an asset.

The Rev. Jacson promptly wrote to Henry Brandreth, whom he obviously regarded as his (unpaid and entirely voluntary) representative in the area, to ask if he could clarify the legal position and what opinion he had of John Lesley. Throughout a correspondence which lasted for many years, Mr Brandreth always replied promptly, with respect and courtesy. On this occasion he sent an extract from the will and spoke quite confidently about John Lesley's abilities despite the fact that he was 'upwards of 70 years'. He mentioned complaints of neglect, saying that when he investigated they were mainly due to the multiplicity of Mr Lesley's business activities and after his (Mr Brandreth's) 'mentioning' the matter, things had been much better.

He suggested that Mr Jacson should write and say that he expected this improvement to continue, but added that most of the complainants were "Dissenters" and "their principal object was to obtain the dismissal of the present master, in hopes that one of their own persuasion might be appointed".

Among the Brandreth papers at the Country Records Office, Bedford, is a letter which, a few weeks later, John Lesley wrote to his son, William, who lived at Warrington, quite near the Rev. Jacson.

He carefully instructed William as to how he should visit the Rev. Jacson, and explain about his father's failing health and the large family which would be homeless unless William was appointed as the next schoolmaster. The letter ends with his sending "love to Nancy and the family" and the signature, "Your affectionate father".

The years passed by, and it was not until 1815 when John Lesley, who was at least 77 years old, became seriously ill, that a young man called George Taylor, from the Coppins School at Market Street (Markyate) applied to the Reverend Jacson for permission to "fill the expected vacancy". He was backed by Henry Brandreth, who on the 23rd October wrote to announce John Lesley's death, describing him as a 'most active man in the county'!

William Lesley also applied for the vacancy, but Henry Brandreth warned that it was only to get control of the house; a third candidate was a Mr Nathaniel Cartwright who. in the trade directories, is described as a 'conveyancer of land' from West St, Dunstable. Throughout October, these three applicants pestered Henry Brandreth. He consistently recommended George

Taylor, who was eventually given the job. The Lesleys, having asked for time to look around for a new home, then started the struggle which was to close the village school for the next seventeen months!

On Sunday 6 November 1815, George Taylor wrote to Rev. Jacson in some panic; the Lesley family had taken the opportunity of most of the village being at "divine service" to uproot shrubs, pull down outbuildings and generally destroy anything of value in the garden of the school house. The letter ends with a frantic postscript that the Lesleys have begun to pull down walls inside the building and he knowns not where it will end!

The next day, Henry Brandreth wrote to explain that "the horrible havoc made on the school property" was caused because the Lesley family, having lost their home, were systematically removing or destroying all the improvements, made by their father. The fruit bushes, the new iron stove, the walls of the "counting house" were all being taken away. (In a letter, Mr Taylor mentions eleven waggon loads of materials being removed!)

Charles, the second Lesley son, then visited Mr Brandreth, who found him a most "artful young man". He blustered and threatened and tried to play off Mr Brandreth against the Rev. Jacson.

Henry Brandreth wrote to inform Mr Jacson that the village families had arranged between themselves to "mount guard at night". He said that "neither your person or property, dear Sir, are in any danger, but I know several in this neighbourhood think otherwise as to myself". He begged that the Rev. Jacson would be very careful as to what he said if Mr Charles Lesley carried out a threat to visit Cheshire and asked Mr Jacson to direct further correspondence to Brandreth's land surveyor, Mr Joseph Tween, at 'Lewsey near Dunstable'.

The postscript starts, "Mr Brandreth being somewhat agitated at what is going forward and being likewise much hurried with business has departed ....." and ends by explaining that Mrs Brandreth is writing the letter for him.

Twelve months later, George Taylor, a trained, experienced teacher and popular in the village, had still not gained admittance to the school! When he wrote asking Mr Jacson to help him, Henry Brandreth was consulted, and recommended consulting a solicitor.

Eventually, Henry Brandreth wrote, "I have at length the satisfaction of informing you that the Lesleys have quitted Houghton and I should be better pleased could I say the neighbourhood". It went on to say that Mr Taylor was going to open the school "tomorrow sennight"; that he was lending Mr Taylor £75 for immediate repairs (to be returned at £10 per annum, no interest) but that they must not spend too much money as the life of the building was now doubtful, and he hinted that there were problems about collecting money from the charity land. He offered to select 20 boys from the "numerous" applicants who were wanting a place.

So the school re-opened on 10 February 1817 and the village, Henry Brandreth and the Rev. Jacson could relax: but not, as it turned out, for long.

In October 1820, three and a half years after the re-opening of the school, Henry Brandreth wrote to the Rev. Jacson, to break the news that following a long illness, George Taylor had died. The school had been kept running by an experienced teacher, Mr Richard Cumberland, and Mr Brandreth and the parishioners considered that "he is in every respect qualified to succeed to this situation".

The death of Mr Taylor prompted Edward French, carpenter, and Joseph Flowers, bricklayer, to point out to Mr Jacson in a polite and very well written letter that they had a joint bill of over £80 outstanding from the repairs that Mr Taylor had ordered for the charity school. Mr Brandreth had paid the original bill to make the building safe, and Mr Taylor had assured them that Mr Brandreth would also settle the further account. However, when Mr Taylor died, they had approached Mr Brandreth who had refused to pay and told them to write to Mr Jacson. The Rev. Jacson was not sympathetic and so they approached the Charity Commissioners when they visited Dunstable but Mr Brandreth heard of this approach -- probably the Commissioners contacted him -- and advised the Commissioners against supporting the tradesmen. The outcome of the matter is unrecorded.

So Richard Cumberland was chosen as the next headmaster. However the Reverend Roger Jacson's heir wrote to "all to whom those present shall come", explaining that he had inherited the responsibility of Thomas Whitehead's bequest and going on to confirm that he had "elected, nominated, constitued and appointed" Richard Cumberland, schoolmaster, to be "Master or Teacher of the Free School" and "to have hold, exercise and enjoy the said Mastership .... during my will and pleasure". This phrase is heavily underlined. He was obviously out to avoid any problems such as those the Lesley family had posed! Despite this care in wording the document, he then included a sentence which the village was to regret bitterly. He wrote that Richard Cumberland was "to receive and take the rent and profits of the said messuage and lands devised by the said Thomas Whitehead......" He makes it quite clear that Cumberland is to take all the income from the land , keep the buildings in a satisfactory state of repair, and then keep the remaining rent as his salary. Mr Jacson kept control of the charity land: Mr Brandreth arranged for him that John Franklin, landlord of the White Horse in Church Street, Dunstable, should be the next tenant and pay £50 p.a. for the 15 acres. This

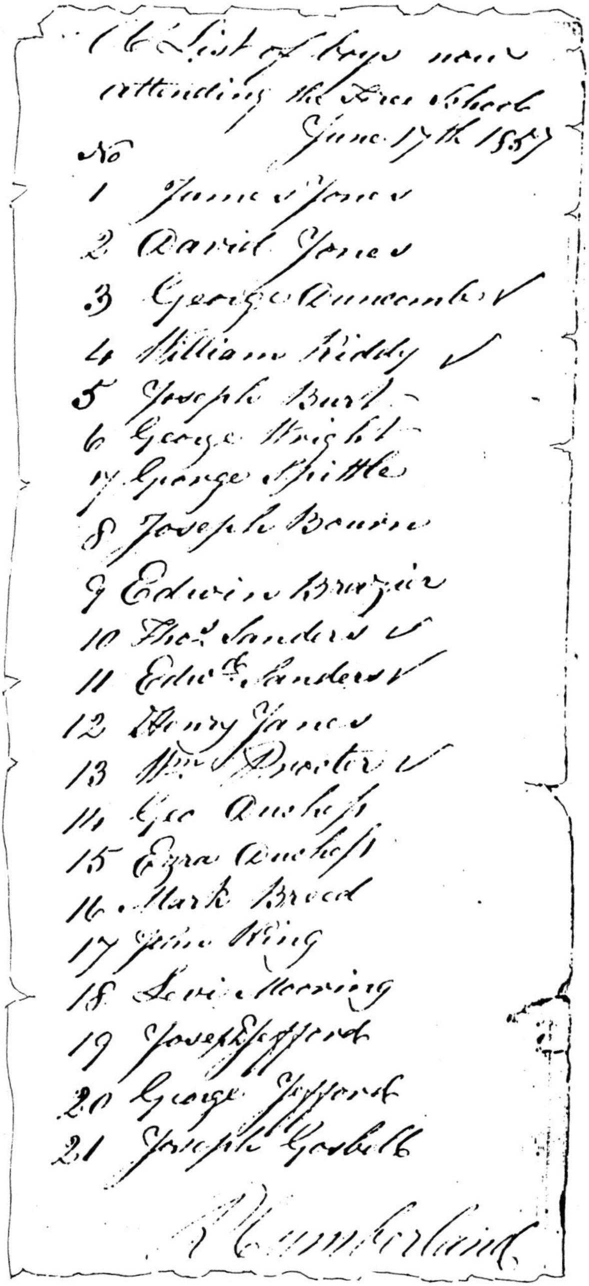

Fig. 38   Richard Cumberland's list of boys attending the Free
          School in 1857. (C.R.O.)

was a high price and with an experienced teacher settled in the school house, which had just been repaired for George Taylor, the school was at last ready for a long settled period.

The Charity Commissioners made several visits to the area, and from their reports we can see that there had been several important changes since the original endowment.

.in 1799, when the open fields had been enclosed, the school had been allotted 1 1/2 acres of land in Sundon Road (the basis of Chantry Farm?) in lieu of common rights.

.by 1822 an average of only 16 boys were attending school because 'young children are kept at home to plait straw for the hat industry.'

.the church catechism was being taught.

Education at the school was free, but by 1820 the master had permission to take additional fee-paying pupils and in addition there is a great deal of evidence that the teachers still had at least one other part-time job during school hours! Cumberland was local surveyor for the gentry, for example.

Although Mr Brandreth interviewed and selected pupils on behalf of Mr Jacson, in practice all who applied were accepted because agricultural wages were so low (about 8s a week) and unreliable, that young children were kept at home to plait straw.

Plait "schools" (which had little or nothing to do with education) thrived in Houghton Regis and on the census of 1841, children as young as 4 are entered as plaiters.

The famous and much respected Chew School had opened in Dunstable in 1715 and was available to

Houghton boys who were strict and regular Church of England attenders. A free uniform was provided, it had excellent masters and above all, gave boys the chance of an apprenticeship grant and tools. So the Chew School competed with the village 'Free School' but, as the boys had to be at least seven years old and able to read from the Bible to be eligible for the Dunstable school, some started their education in the village.

To combat this competition, the 'Free School' took boys at a very young age, some of whom were transferred to the Chew School and others of whom were taken away as soon as they had a basic knowledge of reading and writing and sent out to work. Although the schoolmaster at Houghton had a wide age-range to teach, the number of pupils was favourable by modern standards, a ratio of 16:1.

Richard Cumberland worked for 35 years without any complaints being recorded. Perhaps if he had been left to continue in his own way, the following twenty years would have been equally uneventful, but outside developments intervened.

Like their father before them, the Reverend Jacson Jnr had written to ask Humphrey Brandreth, Henry's son, about the possibility of giving up the Trusteeship and had been warned that the income from the charity land was only £50 per year, and that 'consequently there is no fund from which lawyers can be paid'! So it was not for some years when, having again consulted Mr Brandreth, he sent an application to the Master of the Rolls. On 8th July 1856, the Master of the Rolls ordered that "Charles Roger Jacson.... be released and removed from the office of Trustee....."

Put in his place were,

"Humphrey Brandreth of Houghton House, Esq.

Hugh Smyth, Vicar
John Cook the Elder, Yeoman and Farmer
Michael Cook the Elder, Yeoman
Joseph Tofield, Builder
Edward Barnard, Farmer", six substantial inhabitants of Houghton Regis, as specified in Thomas Whitehead's original will.

Unfortunately for the new Trustees, this turned out to be one of the most difficult years in the history of the school.

When the Reverend Hugh Smyth had been inducted into the vicarage at the end of January, Humphrey Brandreth had been at his London house and Mr Smyth had written to consult him.

The Duke of Bedford had "expressed a wish to have an interview with him" and before this happened he wanted to get Mr Brandreth's view about "the state of the parish". Mr Brandreth's reply has not survived, but the rough copy of an undated letter, written some months before, suggests he was most concerned about the state of education in the parish.

In the 17th century the Free School had been the only school in the area, but gradually more had been built, and in the first half of the 19th century 'British' (Nonconformist sponsored) and 'National' (Church of England sponsored) schools had been built in many towns and villages. Houghton had now slipped behind, and as apart from the few private pupils, education was limited to the twenty poor boys, there was a growing demand for more school places and a higher standard of education. Girls were excluded from the 'Free School' and nonconformists would not attend a school where 'prayer book' based services were enforced.

New schools in the 19th century were either started by the lord of the manor or by subscription, plus

116

grants from the British or National Societies. Humphrey Brandreth knew that they must provide a bigger school; he gave no consideration to the first two methods, and could not ask the National Society for money because he had fallen out with the Vicar!

In his undated letter which was possibly intended for the Rev. Jacson, he puts forward the suggestion that "with a suitable arrangement" the Free School might "be made efficient for the whole parish, both for boys and girls." He goes on to explain that about two years ago he discussed this expansion with Mr Cumberland but, "as I had not a clergyman in the parish who would assist me in attending to the details of the after management, without attempting to give himself airs and perhaps availing himself of the opportunity of throwing his petty spite to the man who had unwittingly offended him; I thought it as well to let the matter stand over....."!

Mr Brandreth did not want the Free School to become a church school "it must be a secular school as it now is, but with more attention to moral instruction" and "without the personal interference of the clergyman"! But it was not simply his quarrel with the Vicar which coloured his views; the National School system included doctrinal religious teaching based on the prayer book, and he felt that that was unsuitable in Houghton, with its strong Nonconformist elements. He was concerned that education was reaching so few. The school was already "badly attended" because "the poor will not send their children to school when they can earn anything at home plaiting."

At Dunstable, in addition to the Chews School, there was a National School (opened in 1839, and now the Priory Church Hall), a British School (opened in 1845, probably in the Temperance Hall, West St), a Wesleyan School, (opened c1812 in a schoolroom behind the chapel in the Square) and a Baptist School (opened c1807 in the Baptist Chapel in West St). These schools, were open to children from Houghton.

There were wealthy nonconformist families in the area and it was likely that if an open, non-selective school were not made available, they might apply for a grant to start a British school. (This in fact did happen, later). Because of this the Trustees had to be careful not to ask for subscriptions for a new building in case they lost control over the school. Mr Brandreth recommended that the present school be made "efficient for the whole parish, both for boys and girls", and only if the increase proved "beyond what the present accommodation will afford" should they consider putting up a new building. If they were forced to build they would "make an arrangement with the present master of the Free School to become the master of the new school" and to include his twenty pupils among the others.

Mr Brandreth's letter gives some idea of the tangled situation that the new Trustees had to face. A "Scheme for the future regulation and management of the Houghton Regis Free School" was drawn up. It started with a list of twenty rules about the choice of Trustees, their behaviour, the necessary meetings and book keeping involved. Rule 17 lists the duties of the treasurer including the collection of the charity rents.

Rule 19 makes the Trustees responsible for repairs to the schoolhouse, premises and other allied expenses. The remaining rules concern the administration of the school: they anticipate that girls will be included, a school mistress employed, and "plain needlework and sewing" added to the subjects taught, but there was no instruction about teaching the catechism. All children of the poor inhabitants should be admitted, if they were of the age of seven years and under the age of fourteen, of good character and not "being afflicted with any infections or other (wise) offensive". Church attendance was not mentioned.

If the new Trustees thought fit, they could charge "head money" not exceeding two pence a week, which would be paid weekly to the schoolmaster, and it was agreed that he could take private paying pupils. But, out of the limited charity income, the Trustees were not only paying for the repairs, fire insurance and sinking fund, but also "all printed books, papers, pens, pencils and other stationery" before they worked out a yearly salary for the master and mistress. Richard Cumberland, after all these years, had lost his control of the charity income; no longer could he rely on his sons (or pupils) to mend fences,paint the school and repair desks etc. and regard the full rent as his personal salary.

Rule 11 required the Trustees to keep a minute book. The first entry is dated October 25th 1856, three months after the committee became the legal Trustees: already things were going wrong! The newly elected treasurer, Humphrey Brandreth, had received a bill for £61 to pay the legal expenses of setting up the new Trusteeship. There were no funds other than the rent from the land, but they could hardly alter the terms of Mr Cumberland's employment without notice, so relucantly they agreed that up until Christmas they would have to leave the rent income as it was, paid in full to the schoolmaster.

At the next meeting, on the 31st December, they reviewed their financial position: the total income from the land was £53 and their basic expenses before repairing the school were nearly £13. Out of the remaining £40 they had to maintain the school building, pay Mr Cumberland and repay their legal debt.

Eventually they resolved that the master's salary should be £35 per year, but when they met on March

12th it was to discuss an impasse which had arisen; Mr Cumberland had not only refused the £35, but had refused to acknowledge the legality of the new "Scheme for regulation and management" and refused to sign the agreement!

The resulting wrangle rocked the village, and lasted for nearly three years. It was clouded with other issues, not least of which was a power struggle to establish a Church of England School! (A National School was in fact built c1857 at the northern boundary of the churchyard).

Much legal advice was taken, stances were struck all round, but in the end common sense seems to have prevailed. A new scheme for the regulation of the charity was filed, some land was mortgaged to relieve the most pressing financial difficulties, and despite everything the school not only continued but gained more scholars. The Charity Commisioners ruled right at the beginning that Mr Cumberland was obliged to agree or might be dismissed, but it is to the credit of the Trustees that they recognised him as a very able schoolmaster and did not consider that course of action.

Richard Cumberland remained as master until he died aged 87 in 1874. He had held the office of schoolmaster for 54 years.

By this time, the old buildings had become very delapidated. In 1875, the situation which had been foreseen by Mr Brandreth arose: there were three schools (the National School, the British School, and the Free School) competing for the insufficient numbers of scholars. The Reverend Hugh Smyth wrote to the trustees, in his capacity of Correspondent to the Managers of the National School, saying that when the present schoolmistress resigned her post on the 1st June 1875, the intention was to close the National School. He then went on to offer the use of the

Fig. 39    Arrowed is the National School, and behind it can be
           seen the tithe barn. "Workhouse Row" is to the right
           of the church.

building unconditionally to the Trustees of the Free
School and at a "nominal or repairing rent" so that a
"first rate school may be provided for the Parish".

This was not intended to be a permanent move.  As
he was also a trustee of the Free School The
Rev. Smyth knew that
a) The old school buildings were badly decayed but —
b) The charity land had increased in value due both to
   the coming of the railway and to the boom in the
   value of the housing land in Dunstable so that the
   trustees were in a position to sell land and raise
   sufficient funds to rebuild the school premises.

Fig. 40 The Free School on Houghton Green, opened in 1881. (C.R.O.)

On 6th September 1875, Asa Heap and his wife were appointed schoolmaster and (part-time) schoolmistress, teaching in the former National School building. Asa Heap was schoolmaster until his death in 1902, another well-respected and able man. Heap was choirmaster at All Saints and there is a strong local tradition that he wrote hymns, but it has not proved possible to trace any of these. The schoolmaster's and schoolmistress' joint salary on his appointment was guaranteed at £100 p.a. £40 of this continued to be income from the charity lands and the rest made up from "head money" and fee-paying pupils.

On 5th July 1877, the trustees wrote to the Charity Commissioners for permission to sell land to fund the building of a new school and schoolmaster's house. Permission was duly obtained, and a new school was built to accommodate 200 scholars, at a cost of £1,250. £3,422.19s.0d was eventually realized on the sale of the charity land.

The new school opened in 1881 and was intended to "provide for the education of the ............. Children of the Parish over 6 years old" and numbers were steadily built up in the temporary building. Fourteen of the boys from Houghton always had their fees remitted in accordance with the original will, as did six boys from the hamlets.

Apparently Mr Heap asked the Trustees to provide the new school with both a clock and a harmonium. The clock was ordered, but the schoolmaster was directed to "get-up an entertainment" to provide the harmonium!

Irreverent than as now, Mr Heap's pupils immortalized him in schoolboy doggerel:

> Asa Heap was a good man,
> He tried to learn you all he can(!)
> Reading, writing and arithmetic,

But he never forgot to give you the stick
When he did he made you dance
Out of England into France,
Into France, out of Spain
Over the hills and back again.

Fig. 41   Interior of the Baptist Chapel, High St., Houghton
Regis. (L.F.)

# CHAPTER 15

## EARLY NONCONFORMISTS

The "Dissenters" who exercised Humphrey Brandreth's mind in the 19th century had a long and distinguished association with Houghton and the local area.

There was an increasing number of people who could not 'conform' with the Church of England because they refused to use the Book of Common Prayer, hence the expression "Nonconformist" or "Dissenter".

At the beginning of the 17th century Houghton church seems largely to have been neglected, but the strength of local feeling can be judged by the events occurring after the appointment of the Reverend Edward Alport to Dunstable in 1609. Alport was a most strict conforming minister; he was so tormented by some of his congregation that he took matters to the Star Chamber in 1616, but seems to have had little satisfaction.

In November 1614, some of his congregation had taken a sheep to the church font and proceeded to name it "Edward Alport" using the "Ceremonie of Baptisme" and then they put the unfortunate animal into the pulpit to preach a sermon!

Three of the offenders had been publicly whipped and excommunicated, but their friends had then disguised them and egged them on to continue to attend services.

Whenever Alport was away, the congregation refused to allow his locum to preach, but invited one of the local Nonconformists instead. Pistol shots were fired over his head. The Churchwardens and constables would not support him.

One night a particularly rowdy crew got thoroughly drunk and went into 'Dunstable Field' to cut most of Alport's corn while it was still green. When he and his servants chased them off, they got a warrant to keep the peace against him!

Subsequently, hearing that Alport had been bailed to keep the peace, another party including some of the Medgate family from Houghton and the Medgate servant Thomas Morgan proceeded to attack the unfortunate Alport. When taken before the Justices Morgan said that "hee was sorry hee had not beate out yr subts (your subjects) braines for then he should have bine well rewarded of Joseph Medgate his master"!

Alport seems to have achieved nothing further by taking his case to the Star Chamber. He accused thirty people plus "others unknown". The defendants pleaded that they had already been punished for sacriligiously baptising the sheep, and there matters seem to have rested as far as the law was concerned.

These events were not isolated. They were part of a pattern occurring in many areas where the struggle for nonconformism was taking place.

Furthermore, it was not just the young and rowdy who were involved, but also respectable businessmen and property owners. Joseph Medgate, who is buried at Houghton, was a man of substance, owning the Ram Inn, several houses in High St. North, a part share in the Bull Inn, and (later, with his son Thomas) Calcutt Farm. He and Thomas are both on the list of accused, as are another son Joseph, Elizabeth and Margery Medgate (probably nieces) from Houghton, Thomas Morgan his servant and at least three other relatives by marriage!

In 1625 the Dunstable advowson was bought by a committee set up to place trained nonconforming ministers into suitably sympathetic parish churches. The Reverend Zachary Symmes was installed as 'curate' and for seven years St Peter's was a nonconformist church. However, the Bishop, suitably outraged, regained control, dismissed Symmes and appointed the Reverend William Pedder; once again a strictly conforming priest was in charge.

As bewildering changes in religion and politics took place nationally and locally, the nonconformist movement gained in strength.

Houghton nonconformists, along with people from a wide area around, attended open air meetings on the Downs. The meetings were often led by Edward Harrison who was to become a leader of the nonconformist movement in South Beds.

In 1643, when Oliver Cromwell was in control of the area. Harrison was appointed lecturer at St Mary's Kensworth and had a large and regular following.

The Restoration of Charles II in 1661 meant that once again only ordained priests could officiate in churches, and the Book of Common Prayer had to be used. There could be no more nonconforming parishes or lay lecturers and attendance at the parish church was once again compulsory.

Edward Harrison moved on to London, and later, Thomas Hayward led the Kensworth Baptists, including the members from Houghton, until his death in 1688. Like other such local leaders he was sometimes called a "hedgerow preacher" in a disparaging way. According to the religious/political climate of the time, he had to hold meetings in the open air, or secretively in private houses; often in considerable danger. He was not, of course, an ordained priest but simply a man called to lead people who wished to worship in their own way, without using the Book of Common Prayer.

In 1676 when James Paddon, Vicar of Houghton, was filling in a religious census, he admitted to 73 nonconformists out of his congregation of 223, but this figure may have been far too low. The official list of 'baptised' members of the Kensworth Baptists in 1675 had included 15 Houghton names; the number of attending members would have been much higher. In addition to the Baptists, a religious survey of 1669 had numbered 40 Quakers at Houghton.

Increasingly the Baptist members met in their local communities. In 1694 William Brittan, yeoman, of Houghton was appointed as Elder, and he played a large role in the development of the Baptist movement in this area. He led meetings in members' homes in both Houghton and Dunstable, and in 1707 he and representatives from other areas bought land and built a "Church House", on the site of the Old Baptist Chapel by Sainsbury's car park in Dunstable. The new chapel served a wide area, including Houghton. By the time of Brittan's death in 1754, this chapel was well established, and many of the Houghton baptists continued to use it for many years. Joseph Mawn, Yeoman, of Kings Houghton was one of the trustees in 1765.

However, when in 1694, the Baptist meeting had decided to elect Wm Brittan as an additional Elder, instead of employing a full-time pastor to cope with the increasing membership, Brother Marsom of Luton had been most annoyed. He had donated a piece of ground in Park Street, Luton, built a chapel on it and appointed a pastor of his own choice. A small group of Houghton and Dunstable Baptists joined him and they attended meetings in Luton for many years. Their numbers grew, and eventually it was decided that this Luton group should have a second meeting place; a site was chosen at Houghton.

The Bunker family of Thorn were among the members, and the new chapel and burial ground was sited on their land near to Thorn Green. Thomas Bunker became the first pastor and the chapel became entirely independent from Luton in 1751. Bunker died in 1769, but the chapel continued with other pastors. Eventually, chapels were built in all the neighbouring villages and then during the winter evenings, services began to be held in a house in Houghton village, just as William Brittan had held them years before. This proved to be so popular that the local committee bought two cottages in Houghton and converted them into a chapel which opened in 1790.

Accommodation soon became a pressing problem – the chapel was too small for the congregation, so they physically moved the original Thorn chapel into Houghton, and rebuilt it, adding an extra 12 feet! It still wasn't big enough for all the members from both Dunstable and Houghton who formed the former Luton group. At first the pastor Daniel Gould held one service in Houghton and another in Dunstable, but in 1836 the two congregations were too big for one pastor to manage so Daniel Gould started a separate chapel in West Street, Dunstable, and a new pastor continued in the village. Funds were raised to build a distinctive new chapel in Houghton High Street in 1864, which was pulled down in the 1970's.

A service is still held at Thorn once a year, and the present Baptist congregation worships in a fine new building on the Parkside Estate, opened in November 1975.

The Quaker movement began locally in a baker's shop in Dunstable which belonged to Edward Chester and his widowed mother. It is thought that Chester may have met the Quaker Richard Hubberthorne in the parliamentary army, because following a visit to

London, Hubberthorne stayed at the bakery on his way home to Lancashire. As a result of this reunion a group of Quaker sympathisers was formed which included Henry Newman Snr, and Henry Newman Jnr, who had a farm at Sewell, also members of the How and King families from Sewell.

The local leader was John Crook, a retired Captain from the parliamentary army, who had an estate called Beckering's Park at Ridgmont. The movement grew very quickly, and George Fox, the founder of the Society of Friends, held a regional meeting at Beckerings Park in 1655 and 1658.

With the return of Charles II in 1660 it was impossible for Quakers to hold public meetings. The problem was that they believed that individuals were "answering that of God in every one" and consequently not only refused to attend the parish church but were against paying ministers, paying for church repairs and paying tithes (which were legally due). When they were taken to court, they refused to swear on oath. Within months of the Restoration the Quakers were being persecuted.

At some stage their South Bedfordshire headquarters moved to Sewell, probably to Newman's Farm, where by 1669 they had least 40 regular attenders, led by John Crook.

Edward Chester, Henry How and Henry Newman Snr were arrested, refused to swear on oath and were sent to prison. In June 1668 the Archdeacon had excommunicated Edward Chester and four others at Dunstable, and in November he excommunicated Henry Newman, Robert King (hemp dresser), Michael Cooke (husbandman), William Francis (labourer), Edward Snoxhill (husbandman) and John Prentice (farmer) from Houghton, all for consistently refusing to attend their parish church.

Henry Newman Jnr was sent to Bedford Goal for refusing to pay 1sld (about 5 1/2p) towards the repair of All Saints. He stayed in jail for two and a half years! Daniel King was also sent to Bedford Goal in 1683 for persistently refusing to take the oath of allegiance, and was imprisoned for 2 1/2 years.

Despite hardships and difficulties, the Quakers leased a plot of land at Sewell which they used first as a burial ground. Robert King was buried there in June 1685 and his death may have been the reason for Daniel King's release from prison. Eventually a meeting house was built, date unknown. It was registered in 1689 after the Toleration Act allowed some degree of freedom of worship, but no release from legal obligations. The Dissenters' meetings were tolerated, but members could still be prosecuted for not attending church and failing to pay tithes!

The Reverend James Paddon at Houghton relied on his share of the tithes (called the small tithes) to supplement his stipend and help support his family. In 1696 he discovered that the unfortunate Daniel King had not paid his small tithes for eight years, a total value of £3. He sent men to impound Daniel's cow in payment. The cow was worth £4.10s, so the Vicar dutifully refunded £1.10s.

Simon Merry had also refused to pay his tithes. £12 worth of hay and unthreshed corn was stolen from his barns, which set off a chain of mysterious accidents to and thefts of the Vicar's livestock, which the villagers attributed to divine retribution!

For a long time the baker's shop remained the Quaker headquarters in Dunstable and was used when inclement weather prevented meetings at Sewell. In 1712 a new meeting house was built in Dunstable, and although Sewell remained very popular as a summer meeting place, in the winter it was left unused.

Repairs became too costly and in 1811 the land and remains of the building were sold.

Eventually, the Dunstable meeting house also closed, and by 1851 local Quakers were meeting in Luton.

Other Nonconformist churches, however, had thrived. The Religious Census of 1851 gives a Houghton population of 2,213. There is a return from the Parish Church of all Saints, and in addition a Baptist church (built in 1803), Westleyan Methodist (built in 1850), Primitive Methodist (built in 1844) and Westleyan Methodist, Chalk Hill (built in 1835) — the numerous "Dissenters" of Mr Humphrey Brandreth's time!

# CHAPTER 16

## THE PUDDLEHILL TURNPIKE

When Dunstable was founded, the Prior had responsibility for the main roads passing through the centre of the town, but Houghton Regis was responsible for the part of Watling Street which passed through the western area of their parish, from the boundary west of Puddlehill and up to the town boundary at what is now Union Street.

Travel was a risky business: lone travellers and those whose business necessitated the carrying of money, such as drovers and carriers, were always at risk and later, stage-coaches were in danger of attack by highwaymen anywhere between towns.

Houghton had responsibility for the "strangers" (travellers) frequently found dead beside the road in the Houghton Regis fields. There is an entry in the parish register dated 13th March 1574 recording that there "was buried a young man founde slayne at Puddel Bridge with his legs bound and sore wounded upon his hed and face" and with a pathetic little detail " and was named at his burial John".

The cost of maintaining the road was another responsibility. In 1285 Edward I complained to the Prior that "the high roads that stretch through your vill aforesaid, are so broken up and deep by the frequent passage of carts, that dangerous injuries continuously threaten those passing by......" He commanded that the Prior should see to it that "each one of you according to his estate and capability shall cause those roads to be filled in and mended....."! The businessmen of Dunstable had a vested interest in maintaining the roads along which they wanted to move their goods to London and the east coast, but the unfortunate Prior had less co-operation when it came to Upper Houghton and Puddlehill.

In 1555 the Highways Act was passed confirming the practice that each man should give four days' labour (later extended to six) or supply a horse and cart to help repair the roads.  Later this became a cash payment ("road rate") collected by the "surveyors of the highway."  These surveyors were elected by the Easter Vestry at the parish church, were answerable to the local JP and were obliged to keep detailed accounts of their expenditure.

This rate was supplemented by endowments, but people were more concerned about their local piece of road than the main highway, as we have seen from the 16th century wills already mentioned.

Traffic increased: more carts, horses and people passed along the main road every year.  In winter Puddle Hill became virtually impassable with mud or snow and the height of the hill to be surmounted can be judged by the sides of the present chalk cutting: a formidable obstacle.  The weight of wagons and the size of their wheels were controlled by law, but even so the road deteriorated and was quite unfit for the springless open-windowed carriages which were in use until the mid 18th century.  In 1768 the rules were changed and, provided a wagon had wheels which were 9 inches broad, it was permissible to use ten horses to pull it up the hill instead of six.  The road between Dunstable and Hockliffe had the dubious honour of being considered one of the worst stretches of highway in England!  Even seasoned travellers complained of

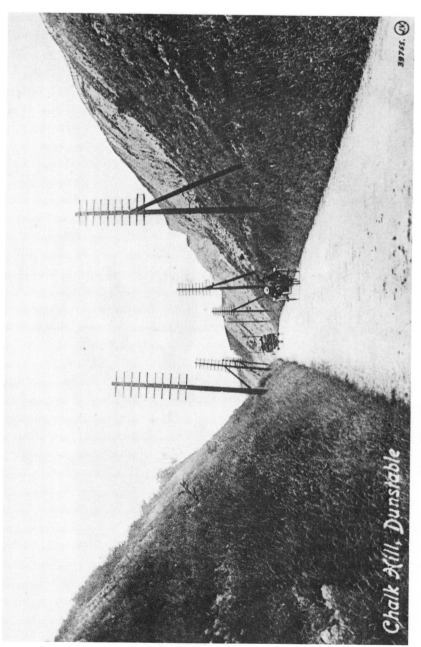

Chalk Hill, Dunstable

397ss.

Fig. 42  The chalk hill at Puddlehill. (L.F.)

the chalk dust in summer, the deep mud in winter and the difficulty and downright danger of traversing the hill.

A bill was read in Parliament as early as 1662 for "repairing and maintaining of the highway called Watling Street in the County of Bedford", but did not get as far as a second reading.

Thirty years later the "Proposal for the Highways" was enacted, enabling committees nationwide to set up barriers and collect tolls from travellers, using the money so collected to help with the upkeep of main highways.

A pike (pole) was put across Watling Street near Sewell Turn in about 1706 and a committee of local landowners formed to administer the 'Puddlehill Trust'. The Trust was conscientious and made several attempts to improve their part of the road. Fifteen years after the formation of the committee, Daniel Defoe remarked on the "handsomely repaired" section of road between the top of the hill and Hockliffe.

However, turnpikes caused traffic jams as coaches, waggons, riders, flocks of sheep and herds of cows waited to pass. They were also, in many cases, less successful financially than had been expected. The costs of keeping up the repairs was high, loans had to be serviced and the system was vulnerable to dishonesty and the vagaries of the weather: a heavy fall of snow for example could cause burdensome debt both by loss of revenue and the cost of clearing.

In the case of the Puddlehill Trust there was also the obstacle of the chalk hill itself. In an attempt to avoid the summit a road was laid out round the south west side of the hill. It started near the present French's Avenue and came out near the present Chalk Hill Garage. It cost £16,000 and was opened in 1782. Travellers could use either route, joining together as they reached the toll-gate. The 'serpentine' road proved to be a temporary solution and a not very successful one. By 1820 the diversion had long been abandoned and was sold to Henry Brandreth for £20! Because of this change of route the toll gate was moved close to Kates Hill near the present turn off for Toddington.

Puddlehill was on the main route to Holyhead on which coach trade was fast increasing: by 1830 up to 80 coaches passed through Dunstable each day. Something had to be done about Puddlehill.

Thomas Telford had been consulted in 1810, but no government funds were immediately forthcoming. The Trust started to cut through the ridge of chalk which was Puddlehill to a depth of 50 feet. They had borrowed £6,440 to do this work. Mr Provis, Telford's assistant, visited Dunstable and reported to Telford that the Dunstable end of the turnpike was in an excellent state of repair. He said that, on average, "seven labourers were employed in winter and twelve in summer digging, carrying and laying nearly 3,000 loads of gravel and stone" each year.

In 1830 Telford himself visited Dunstable, staying at the Sugar Loaf with Sir Henry Parnell and another committee member. The problem was that competition was looming for the lucrative coach trade: not only were people experimenting with steam carriages which would run along the very roads the coaches now used, but even more serious, a railway line was expected between London and Birmingham in the next few years. If horse-drawn coaches were going to compete with this sort of opposition, nothing short of digging a road through the entire hill would do. In 1833 a serious accident lent weight to this argument, when the Liverpool Express was overturned while crossing the hill; one man was killed and several people seriously injured.

In 1836 Parliament voted £10,000 for "lowering Chalk Hill" and work was begun the following year. it is ironic to think that as the men dug away the chalk cutting at Puddlehill, the railway was being laid from London to Birmingham. By 1837 the line was completed as far as Tring, and in 1839 was open to Birmingham. The coaching boom was over. In June 1836, 32 coaches passed through the toll-gate, in 1837, 28 coaches passed through, in 1838, 12, and in 1839 only the Greyhound and the Albion were still running regularly through the town. Local traffic would however have continued to use the Puddlehill road, and the Trust was able to sell the right to collect tolls as late as 1868. In the 1870's Turnpike Trusts ended with the transfer of road maintenance to other authorities.

# CHAPTER 17

## INDUSTRY AND SERVICES

In 1657, a London to West Chester stage coach was advertised, running three days a week; it was the forerunner of many such services. By 1830 up to 80 coaches passed through Dunstable each day, and the town was full of inns to provide for the needs of travellers and horses.

There was an enormous demand for 'post' horses: those used by the mail coaches had to be changed frequently. Inns which specialized in the posting trade needed a great deal of stabling and land, and the Houghton land north east of the Duke of Bedford's Arms (now Grove House) was used for grazing.

The Bull in Upper Houghton was a very large courtyard inn, with a great deal of grazing land. One piece of 15 1/2 acres stretched across to Leighton Gap (West St), and much of Edward Street, Dunstable, is built on the Bull's fields. It was first called the Prince's Arms, and then the Red Hart, and became known as the Bull in 1649. John Byng stayed there in 1789 --- he and his friend were offered duck for supper but, not unnaturally, refused having seen them "dead or dying" in every part of the garden!

The inns and coaching trade provided a ready market for Houghton's produce of all kinds, but growing alongside the activites connected with agriculture and

139

horse chandlery was the straw plait industry. In 1689 straw hat makers from Bedfordshire, Buckinghamshire and Hertfordshire had petitioned Parliament against the use of wool caps. They claimed that 14,000 people lived solely by making straw hats, but "solely" was probably rhetorical licence, because in the 17th century plaiting and straw hat making was a cottage industry mainly for women and children.

Straw hats, baskets, toys, artificial flowers and novelties of all kings could be sold as souvenirs to the travellers passing through Dunstable and upper Houghton, and by the time the coach trade dwindled, plaiting for the hat-making industry in Dunstable and Luton was well established in Houghton Regis.

There was also a special kind of marquetry produced locally. Straw was split, flattened, polished and dyed. It was then pasted on to thin strips of paper and when it had dried it was cut out and used as decoration for baskets and workboxes.

James Holt's family, living in the High Street at Houghton in 1871 bought straw from the farmers and scraped, cleaned and graded it. The children tied it up in bundles and it was sold to customers ready for plaiting. Any surplus was sold in the Wednesday plait market at Dunstable. The Turvey family, of King St., Houghton, drove round the villages to buy scores (20 yard lengths) of finished plait, which were then sold to the bonnet sewers. However, by taking their own plait to the market on Wednesday, plaiters could command the top prices.

Whole families were engaged in plaiting in Houghton as· elsewhere. Arthur Young, who travelled round the country in about 1804, was told that in the season, six year old children could earn 1s6d to 2s0d per week, and by the time they were ten, hard-working children could earn 12s a week. It is worth noting that this was the top agricultural wage for a skilled man at the time, so no wonder children were kept at home to plait instead of being sent to school!

According to the 1851 census for Houghton, in the 100 or more cottages between Townsend Farm amd Green Farm (on the green), at least 183 plaiters are recorded, the youngest being three years old. There were also a handful of bonnet sewers and on that one side of the road alone there was the straw dealer, James Holt, and two plait dealers Richard Tearle and William Axtell. Samual Axtell, William's father, was a grocer and poorer families could barter their plait for provisions in his and other shops or at the pubs.

There were also four ladies recorded as "school mistresses". The plait "schools" were dismal affairs, more to do with organised child-minding than education. They were cold and cramped. Each child paid a fee of about 2d a week, so to equal an experienced plaiter's wage of about 10s, the schoolmistress would have had to take 60 children! They usually took fewer than this but even so the inspectors often found that there were was no instruction in reading and writing and Mrs. Poulter and Mrs Tompkins, two of the Houghton schoolmistresses did not even know how to plait! In a cottage in Church Place -- the houses in front of All Saints -- a Sam Poulton described himself as a "plaiting schoolmaster" and his wife and two sons as plaiters.

Early in the morning the children, some as young as 3 or 4, were sent off to the plait school with a bundle of straw which they were expected to turn into finished plait by dinner time. The same thing happened in the afternoon, and the older children were expected to finish yet another score of plait at home in the evening.

When the factory inspectors visited Houghton in 1869 they found that every cottage in the village contained plaiters but that also agriculture continued as before. In the hundred or so cottages already mentioned, in addition to the 183 plaiters there were also 60 agricultural labourers. In the village itself were Townsend Farm, Green Farm, Tithe Farm, Chantry Farm and several outlying ones, as well as the farms at Bidwell, Calcutt, Thorn and Sewell.

"Upper" West Street, Dunstable, was in Upper Houghton; it was lined with houses standing in their own large gardens. The factory owners lived there, as did professional men attracted by the prosperity of Dunstable.

By 1870, however, plaiting for the hat trade was in decline. After import duties were lifted the market was flooded with cheap foreign plait, and Houghton plaiters saw the price commanded for a score of plait fall from 1s or more before duties were lifted, down to 3d by 1900.

In the 26 cottages of the hamlet at Puddlehill, the 1851 census shows that there were 82 straw plaiters but when the market for plait became depressed, they turned to smallholding and duck breeding.

In the 1881 census for Houghton we see an increase in the number of bonnet sewers and in the directory for 1877 Thomas Bartlett is shown as a straw hat manufacturer in the village. The bonnet-sewing was done as outwork and was poorly paid. When electric sewing machines were brought into use, the outworkers hired them for 2s6d per week, and Bedfordshire County Council arranged classes in the village so that people could learn to use them.

In Dunstable, as straw hats became less fashionable and the industry became mechanised, the hat factories began to close or move to Luton. There were four left by 1900 and none by 1931. In Houghton, however, the directory for 1898 shows Mrs. Goosey's hat factory in Bedford Road , Houghton, and soon after

Cumberland's opened in King Street. Hat making and hat trimming went on in a small way in the village until comparatively recent times.

As the hat industry declined in importance,new industry took its place on the outskirts of Houghton Regis.

When the railway line to Leighton Buzzard opened in 1848, and that to Luton in 1858, both stations were actually in Houghton, one being in High Street North and the other in Church Street.

In 1891 Waterlow's printing works came to Upper Houghton near to Watling Street, and on the southern edge of the parish Harrison Carter opened their engineering works on the Luton Road in 1894. During the ten years from 1891 to 1901, Houghton's population rose from 2,187 to 2,608 respectively, a measure of the development taking place in the area.

Fig. 43  Waterlow Ltd.'s printing works. (O.R.)

The boundaries of the parish were changed in 1907, so that much of the industry coming in was now sited just outside of Houghton, but still provided employment for the villagers. Quite apart from industrial work, the steady expansion of Dunstable meant that there was an increased demand for Houghton's fresh food and other produce.

At Sewell and Blows Downs, J.B. Forder developed lime works which he sold to Blue Circle Cement in 1912. Blue Circle opened a large cement works by what was Townsend Farm and began to cut away the chalk from Puddlehill in 1920. In later years, the huge chimney and processing plant dominated the skyline of Houghton Regis.

The rising population and local development meant that the Surveyors of the Parish had to give thought to matters such as sewage disposal, water supply and so on. In 1856 there is a map of the village showing the main sewer running down the High Street! The Surveyors proposed to build a covered extension to the main sewer with "monies arising from the sale of Houghton Regis Church pond". The extension is in fields just beyond what is now Poynters Road, emptying into a "clear running stream called washing ditch"!

In Dunstable, the subject was not tackled until the 1890's, when pipes were connected up along the four main roads with the intention of depositing the sewage into a pond at Parks Farm behind Kingsbury! A Government enquiry in 1900 forced the authorities to abandon that plan, and a sewage disposal plant was built at the western end of Houghton Regis parish, near to Sewell, which still serves Dunstable and a part of Houghton.

A subscription was raised to bring a gas supply in to Houghton in 1863, but when it came to a piped water supply in the village, there was great opposition.

Fig. 44  The workforce at the turn of the century at J.B. Forder's lime works at Sewell.  (M.D.)

Fig. 45  The Blue Circle cement works at Houghton Regis before the chimney was demolished.  (H.B.)

Nobody wanted to pay for a commodity which could be had freely everywhere in the village.

The proposed water rates were to be 8s a year for a cottage, 14s for a public house, 30s for a farm , 16s for a private house and a massive £20 for Houghton Hall.

In 1878 the Clerk to the Luton Union wrote to the Overseers of the Poor of the Parish of Houghton Regis, asking them to summon a meeting "at your early convenience" to discuss the matter, pointing out that the provision of piped water would be self-financing from the rates and containing a barbed post-script noting that if the Sanitary Authorities did have to take matters into their own hands, there would be the added cost of " a paid official to see after the distribution and also a Collector for the Rates". So, reluctantly, the Overseers agreed and piped water reached the village.

The cottages in front of the Church were known as "Workhouse Row", and on the end was a small building known locally as the "cage" or the village lock-up, where when necessary felons and drunks were detained for the night. The story is told of one woman being taken from the lock-up to Luton Police Station in a trap. The horse suddenly took fright and bolted out of control, breaking the shafts and tipping the prisoner and her escorts unceremoniously out into the road!

Fig. 46 "Workhouse Row" with the lock-up (arrowed) at the end. (C.R.O.)

# CHAPTER 18

## CHURCH AFFAIRS

The Churchwardens' account book for 1714-1858 gives an interesting insight into the period. There are the expected disbursements for washing the surplices, cleaning the clock, buying communion bread and wine, painting the sundial, buying brooms and mops, repairing the weathercock, but in addition they were responsible for the control of various kinds of vermin and these loom large in the accounts; for example:

| 1715 | Pd to Richard Hawkins for a polecat | 9d |
| 1716 | 4 doz sparrows | 8d |
| 1717 | 3 hedgehogs | 1s 0d |
| 1725 | Sparrows | 1s 4d |
| 1735 | Vermin | 13s 01/2d |
| 1768 | Sparrows | 15s 2d |

The Churchwardens were responsible for looking after the welfare of strangers and travellers and this also is reflected in the accounts.

| 1733 | A poor man with a letter of request | 2d |
| 1735 | Paid to an old soldier with a printed pass | 6d |
| 1753 | Three poor sailors with a pass | 1s 0d |
| 1755 | Straw for Elizabeth Field for a bed | 4d |
| 1756 | Paid to poor woman with a child to send her away(!) | 6d |

1759    Paid to Widdo Webb for carpenters work
        done after her husband's decease by John
        Cook                                        6s 0d

In a lighter vein there are also disbursements for
joyful occasions:

1761    Pd to John Todd for ringing when King
        came to Crown                              10s 0d
        Pd to Mr Boushire for beer for the
        ringers on the King's wedding day          10s 0d
1767    Beer for the ringers on Christmas Eve      5s 0d

We have a somewhat jaundiced first hand account of
the appearance of the church in the 19th Century,
written by "W.A." in "Bedfordshire Churches" (no. 32)
and dated October 12th 1846.

"The chancel roof is ceiled, and whitewashed so
smoothly and thickly, as not to leave a vestige of its
architectural ornaments, except two corbels, which may
possibly be original, but they are too loaded with
paint to decide. The chancel arch is blocked up,
presenting on one side whitewashed boards, and on the
other, a most execrable painting which but for its
situation, we should have taken for a burlesque. The
remains of an apparently good screen are used to
support this unsightly object. There is a tablet
which should be in any other part of the Church. A
miserable coat of arms with the emblems of mortality
at the top, mocking this odious pageantry, and the
clumsy tablet just mentioned, are the only attempt at
ornament, and do not afford the slightest consolation
for the absence of those beautiful decorations that
have either been destroyed, or concealed by the cold
mass of whitewash, which disfigures this holy
building. This portion has been selected to contain
two square pews higher and more objectionable than
those in the body of the Church.

In the nave is a wooden roof in good order, a part

of the original yet remains, the corbels which support it are so thickly plastered up, as utterly to defy description. The whole is well whitewashed, and the columns are smeared with paint.

The pulpit, reading pew, and clerk's desk are on the approved auctioneer's system. Their removal, and the abolition of the latter, for which there can be no necessity, would be a great improvement. There is a gallery which has the negative merit of not excluding the western light. Happily as yet there is no organ. Hat pegs disfigure the north aisle only. The pews are all enclosed, which is the more absurd, as we understand that they are all free. The font, a very good specimen, is placed in an obscure corner, instead of standing boldly in its proper place. A beautiful rose window, sadly disguised, in the south aisle, overlooks a portion of the church, partitioned off as a lumber-room and dust hole, which surprises us, as very praiseworthy attention is paid to the neatness and cleanliness of the rest of the building. The chancel is slated. The churchyard is a grazing ground for sheep, which were trampling down the graves unprotected from their ravages."

The gallery mentioned as being at the west end of the church was built in 1774, rebuilt and enlarged in 1842 to accommodate the schoolchildren and removed in 1856.

In the north aisle is a window erected in 1864 to the memory of Minna, the eldest child of the Rev. and Mrs. Hugh Smyth, Vicar. Nearly 1,000 persons contributed towards the cost of this window. The subject portrayed is "Christ blessing little children", and the faces of the four children in the group are taken from photographs of the Vicar's children, the one with a headband of wild flowers being Minna herself. At the time, this was one of the first uses of photography in stained glass work and as such is a notable feature.

In the church porch is a very delapidated notice
commemorating a grant of £30 from the Incorporated
Society for Promoting the Enlargement, Building and
Repairing of Churches and Chapels. The grant was
"towards reseating and restoring this church. All the
seats are for the free use of the Parishioners
according to the law". On this occasion the old box
pews were largely done away with, and the present open
pews put in.

The following year, 1879, an enormous programme of
restoration was undertaken. The chancel was rebuilt
on its original foundations, reusing much of the old
materials. This was followed in 1892 by a restoration
of the tower which cost £1,100; a staggering sum which
would all have been raised by public subscription.

In 1913 Mrs Mary Whitford Cartwright, a
parishioner, left land in a will to the Vicar and
Churchwardens of Houghton Regis, with certain
restrictions on its sale. This bequest enabled the
P.C.C. to build its first daughter church in the
Dunstable part of the parish. The first Christ Church
was a temporary construction in Union Street,
nicknamed the "tin tabernacle". In 1937 a more
permanent Mission Church with dual purpose hall was
built on the corner of Clifton Street. This Church,
with a succession of curates-in-charge, thrived and
built up a number of active groups which came to an
end with the parish boundary changes in 1961. Christ
Church was let to the Rector of Dunstable for a
peppercorn rent but finally ceased to be used for
worship in 1965. The altar and fittings were
transferred to the Parish Church of Houghton Regis,
and some items including an altar are there to this
day. Poor Christ Church suffered the indignity of not
only being closed as a church, but also becoming a
Christmas cracker warehouse until it was partly
damaged by fire. The sad story of Christ Church only
ended when the new Vicar, Geoffrey Neal, evolved a
scheme in keeping with the original will to sell the

site for a sheltered housing scheme (now named Christ
Church House), and the funds were used to build hall
facilities in the tower of the parish church. A
notice in the church recalls these events.

Fig. 47   The interior of Christ Church, Dunstable.(D.H.H.S.)

# CHAPTER 19

## SOME HOUGHTON WORTHIES

Above the old vestry door of the church, there is an extract from the will of William Strange, dated 7th June 1664. William Strange owned a farm of 140 acres in Houghton, let at the time to Edward Snoxell, one of a well known family who also farmed at Totternhoe and Dunstable. Strange bequeathed the rent charge of "ten pounds stirling" to be used for the benefit of the poor of the parish "such as are aged, impotent, weak, sickly, poor Housekeepers or others that frequent God's ordinances and Divine Services and not Quakers or common Beggars".(!)

In 1879 the payments were being made in sums of 2s6d for communicants and 1s6d for non-communicants. Even then, the bequest was heavily subsidised by other charitable giving. Inflation finally overtook the payments and nowadays the £10 is merged into a general charitable fund.

A famous weather man, Richard Inwards, was born in Houghton Regis in 1840. His father had a grocery and provision business in Houghton High Street. Inwards began work as an insurance agent, but was later apprenticed as a mining engineer. In 1861, at the age of 21, he was elected to a Fellowship of the Royal Astronomical Society. In 1862 he joined the Meteorological Society and remained a member for 75 years (!) until his death in 1937. He was President of the Society 1894/5. He travelled extensively, managing mines in Bolivia and Spain; he reported on mining enterprises in Norway, Austria, Mexico, Spain, Portugal and England.

From his early youth he collected sayings about the weather from all over the world. By the age of 28, he had published his notable book "Weather Lore". Inwards' book contained some of his collection of sayings - one local example is:

"Well, Duncombe, how will be the weather?"
"Sir, it looks cloudy altogether;
And coming across our Houghton Green,
I stopped and talked with old Frank Beane.
While we stood there, sir, old Jan Swain
Went by, and said he knowed 'twould rain;
The next that came was Master Hunt,
And he declared he knew it wouldn't;
And then I met with Farmer Blow --
He plainly said he didn't know.
So sir, when doctors disagree,
Who's to decide it -- you or me?"

Inwards was Editor of the Journal of the Royal Meteorological Society for 20 years, and published works on a variety of subjects: a biography, a book about the monuments and people of the Andes, articles in learned magazines such as the "Horological Journal" and so on. He was obviously a man of wide ranging interests. He never married, and lived in London in later life.

There were two windmills at Houghton Regis until the end of the last century. One of them was at the end of the present Mill Lane and remains of it can still be seen. The second was in Houghton High Street at the corner of what is now White House Close. It was opposite Tithe Farm. The mills were both worked for generations by the Freeman family.

Fig. 48  The windmill in Mill Lane. (C.R.O.)

156

Josiah Freeman (usually known as "Cyre") was born in 1837, and he was the last miller to work the mill in the High Street. He was noted for the fact that he could lift a one hundredweight sack of corn in each hand!

His sister Rebecca (born in 1831) married John Cooper, and their son Charles was brought up in the 18th century White House in Houghton High Street. Charles emigrated to America at the age of 22, where he subsequently became a prominent judge. He had two sons, Arthur and Frank, the latter being born in Montana in 1901. The brothers were sent to Dunstable, to be educated at Dunstable Grammar School. Later, after his return to America, Frank changed his name to "Gary" Cooper and became famous as a film star. He died in 1961.

As a boy, Gary frequently visited his cousin Laura Freeman who lived next door to the White House. Laura was one of the longest serving teachers at the school on the Green, and taught many Houghton youngsters to read and write. She was Gary Cooper's godmother, and they were firm friends.

The White House was pulled down in the 1950s and White House Close was built in its grounds.

Like all villages Houghton could lay claim to many characters of local renown, as well as the nationally famous.

The Neale family was reputed to be the tallest in Bedfordshire; Mr Charles Neale ran the Bricklayers Arms, which was beside the old Tithe Farm building on the site of the present Shopping Centre. He and two of his sons were well over six feet tall, and his daughter Elsie was reputed to be 6'10". There was an enormous tree opposite the village green known as the Pound Tree because it stood on the site of the village pound (where stray animals were kept to be claimed).

Fig. 49   The Pound Tree opposite the green. (S.B.)

This tree shows clearly on a map dated 1762. When it became unsafe, it was the Neale brothers who took down the tree.

A long serving Churchwarden of All Saints was Francis (Frank) Buckingham. He gave the church a silver chalice and paten in 1960 to mark his 21 years' service as Churchwarden. Frank was very interested in the history of the church and wrote the first booklet to be published on the subject. He was a music teacher and lived in one of the cottages built by the Duke of Bedford, behind the site of the old Pound Tree.

Another character well known to the whole village was Lol Bright who died in 1976. His father had been a groom at Houghton Hall and Lol himself was a grave digger and unofficial guardian of the churchyard for many years right up to his death; just one of Houghton's many redoubtable inhabitants!

# CHAPTER 20

## THE TWENTIETH CENTURY

The changes which took place in Houghton over the early years of this century tended to be gradual ones.

The Brandreth family sold Houghton Hall to Col. (later Sir) Dealtry Part in 1913. He lived there until well after the Second World War, during which time he became Lord Lieutenant of the County and Master of the Hertfordshire Hunt. The hunt kennels were nearby, next to the schoolmaster's house on the green; people used to walk over from Dunstable to look at the dogs via Dog Kennel Walk. Sir Dealtry's hunters were kept in the stables next to the Hall.

During the first World War soldiers were camped on the green, and they used to practise digging trenches in Drury Lane.

In the High Street, the old Kings Arms was pulled down between the Wars, and the present building put up in about 1936. There was a large pond opposite the Chequers, and this was filled in somewhen in the thirties. The pond had been a favourite play spot for the village children, the boys all fished for tiddlers and fell in quite frequently. Farmers could drive their carts down a slope on one side and out again on the other. This was done to swell the wooden wheels and prevent the iron rims from coming off, although it did clean the carts as well.

Fig. 50     Houghton High Street around the turn of the century. (C.R.O.)

Fig. 51     The stable mews next to the Hall, converted into private houses. (O.R.)

Up until the 1950's there were few changes in the village scene. Houghton had its church and chapels, pubs and small village shops, its almshouses, farms and a 15th century tithe barn. The village green, overlooked by Houghton Hall, the school, the schoolmaster's house and the 18th century Red House must have been typical of rural England as its best. The well kept cricket ground was edged with beech trees and at that time there was very little traffic to disturb the peace.

Across the road were 19th century cottages built for the servants at Houghton Hall, and a little way past the green was the old thatched Crown Inn, still there and beautifully maintained. Many of the shops and cottages lining the High Street were 17th century. Among those of this period that remain are Kirsty's and Sandy's Hairdressers (the oak beam construction can easily be seen inside the building), Odman's, Tudor Motorcycles and part of Regis Motors next door. Vane Cottage in Poynters' Road, Dene Hollow in Sundon Road and several other buildings are of this period or slightly later.

Two World Wars made little physical difference to the appearance of the village. At the school on the Green, Mr Harold A Brown was the schoolmaster from 1903 to 1930. Very little of the first World War disturbs the even tenor of the school at the beginning of hostilities although on 3rd March 1915 there is an entry in the logbook, "The bigger girls have now completed half a dozen pairs of socks besides mittens for the troops at the front; the wool for which had been bought by the children's own subscriptions", and on the 26th May "The school has collected seven shillings for the Empire Day Fund for providing comforts for the Troops".

Two years on, however, the War intrudes much more. In January 1917 a lesson was given to the children on "The Inadvertent disclosure of Military Information as

Fig. 52    The old King's Arms.    The banner reads "Long May They Reign".    (M.G.)

requested by the Education Committee"! One wonders what the "average attendance of 60" made of it! A War Savings Association was started in the school in April.

On several afternoons in September and October of the same year there was an afternoon's holiday to enable the children to gather blackberries under the scheme set up by the "Food Production Department" (Ministry of Agriculture) for harvesting the blackberry crop to make jam for the Army and Navy. A total of 1cwt 26lbs of blackberries was picked. Other entries record that on 16th November "the boys have collected 1/2 ton of chestnuts", presumably for home consumption, and on the 23rd "the children have agreed to devote their Prize Money this year to the British Red Cross". In June 1918 the children subscribed "11/- to the Over Seas Club Fund for comforts to soldiers", and once again, blackberrying took place in the September and October; this time 2cwt 13lbs was collected!

On Armistice Day 1918, the entry notes that only 50 out of 76 children were present. The school was reopening after a most serious influenza epidemic and there is no mention of the end of the World War.

The most noticeable feature in reading the log-books is that the children are frequently absent because of epidemics of diptheria, measles, chickenpox, whooping-cough, mumps and scarlet fever. It was during the War years that children began to be weighed regularly, and to have their height noted; January 1920 is the first record that the School Dentist "examined the teeth of the children aged 5 to 8 years". By the time of the Second World War, the School Dentist is a regular feature of school life, together with the Health Visitor and the School Doctor. Attendance is regularly over 90%.

Mr Sidney Chaperlin was another long-serving

Fig. 53    The pond formerly opposite the Chequers. (H.B.)

THE GREEN — HOUGHTON REGIS

Fig. 54    Sheep grazing on the green.    The Pound Tree
is to the right. (C.R.O.)

schoolmaster, resident from 1930 to 1954 and was therefore in charge throughout the Second World War.

In January of 1939, he was concerned in carrying out a survey of accommodation in the village under the Government Evacuation Scheme.

The entry for 18th September reads,

"School re-opened today a week later than the holiday arranged, owing to the outbreak of hostilities between England and Germany. This resulted in the evacuation of children from London, and the delay in opening was due to the time necessary to complete arrangements for their education. In this school the Infants Department of the Lancing St London County Council School has been accommodated, together with a number of children evacuated with their parents from London and other districts. With new admissions, there is now a roll of 156". The former roll had been 97. "Additional staff in the persons of Mrs Branegan, Head Mistress, and Miss Chodle of the Lancing St Infants Department and Mrs Rippin and Miss Faulkner of the Senior Girls Department are at present working in the school".

The children arrived at the green by the coach-load, and tumbled out carrying their gasmasks in their distinctive square boxes. Gasmasks were meant to be carried all the time at the beginning of the War, and everyone had to practise wearing them. They smelt horribly of rubber, and made a rude noise at the sides if the wearer breathed too hard.

The numbers of evacuees being accommodated vary, and the roll quickly drops to a more reasonable 103 or less. In March 1940, the Diocesan Inspection mentions "children from St Pancras Church of England School, London, together with their teachers" and on 14th May 1940 the entry reads:

Fig. 55    The Crown Inn. (A.J.)

Fig. 56    Vane Cottage. (B.M.)

"Re-opened at 9 am today instead of 15th inst, a Royal Proclamation having cancelled Bank Holiday and an order being issued for all schools to reopen owing to the situation arising from the invasion of Holland, Belgium, and Luxembourg by the Germans. 19 children from the Open Air School, Euston Square, until recently accommodated in the Old National School room, were added to the number of Official Evacuees now in attendance at this school".

On 1st July, "protective measures in connection with possible air raids" are being discussed, and by 26th July the "Refuge Rooms" were ready in which it was claimed the children could be settled in 30 seconds. From September onwards, the Refuge Rooms were in frequent use, the Air Raid Alert sounding 2 or 3 times a week.

On 8th May 1845 "the school was closed on these 3 days (May 8,9,10th) to celebrate the Victory in Europe, May 8th being known as VE Day".

The school was known as the Houghton Regis Free (or Charity) School. At the implementation of the Butler Act it became (officially) a Church of England school, and in 1956 it took the name of its founder to become the Whitehead Voluntary Primary School. At this time Mr Frank Faiers was the Headmaster, Mr Chaperlin having retired at the end of 1954 after 24 1/2 years' service.

In 1967 Mr Faiers supervised the move from the site on the green, in use for over 300 years, to the present spacious site to the north of the church, on part of what had been Rectory land, and to new purpose-built premises. Sadly, Mr Faiers died in February 1972 after a long illness.

A disastrous fire destroyed the building in 1975. The Trustees made an enormous effort and using part of the Thomas Whitehead funds, managed to rebuild the

Fig. 57     The present Thomas Whitehead V.A. Lower School.
            (D.H.H.S)

school completely within a year, taking the opportunity to add a Nursery Unit, in 1977 the first to open in the area.

In the foyer of the present school can be seen the charred remains of a cross, a relic of the fire and originally given to commemorate the Headship of Frank Faiers.

In 1959, the population of Houghton Regis was 3,750. Nowadays the population is estimated at between 16,000 and 20,000 and most of the building in the town and its outskirts has taken place in the last thirty years.

In the early 60s Tithe Farm Estate, a London overspill development, was built on what had been the Rectory land. Later, a modern shopping centre was built on the site of the old National School and the Tithe Farm building. At first it was hoped to include the ancient barn intact into this development, but it was found to be in too rotten a condition and so was demolished.

Along the High Street, buildings were demolished to make way for warehousing, factory and commercial development. In 1969 another large area to the east of Sundon Road was built on and became the Parkside Estate. This area included the site of the old Chantry Farm. In addition to the public housing and commercial development, there was also a great deal of private housing being built, all contributing to a huge increase in population and the provision of services that this entailed.

By 1970 All Saints Church found itself at the centre of a rapidly growing "new town development scheme" with extra housing estates planned in the eastern part of the parish. To meet that developing situation and the expanding population a daughter church was planned in 1972 to be called St Thomas'; its first minister was the Rev C W J Samuels who stayed for four years.

The congregation met to begin with in the local schools and with the new Baptists' church on Parkside Drive. However, from 1976 when the new Vicar the Rev Geoffrey M Neal had appointed the Rev Guy E Buckler as an assistant curate to continue a special ministry on Parkside, the church of St Thomas met regularly in one room of the curate's house at 7 Enfield Close. This situation continued for ten years. The P.C.C. and Vicar have now purchased land in the Parkside area and with special grants have planned a purpose built new parsonage house with a meeting room annexed. St Thomas will remain therefore part of the single parish of Houghton Regis and as a daughter church, together with All Saints, provide a wider ministry for the whole area.

Since 1980 Houghton Regis has been a town, with its

Fig. 58   St. Thomas' Family Communion being celebrated
at 7 Enfield Close. (G.B.)

own Mayor and Councillors.   It is significant that on
the Mayor's chain of office is a picture of All Saints
Church, the oldest building in the parish.

Unfortunately, modern air pollution and the weather
have combined to ravage the exterior of the building
and in the second half of the 80s the church faces an
urgent and major restoration programme.   Delay in its
implementation will mean a gradual closing down and
disuse of parts of what is a Grade 1 listed building;
let us hope that the town can find within itself the
means to rescue and restore this link with its long
and noble heritage.

Royal Houghton has survived and prospered in many
difficult circumstances over the centuries; the
enormous growth of the area in the last three decades
has undoubtedly presented a challenge equal to any
faced in the past.   I am sure that the new town will

not only meet that challenge in its own shrewd and inimitable way, but make from it a Houghton of which we can continue to be proud.

Fig. 59   A fair on the green at the turn
of the century.  (H.B.)

# BIBLIOGRAPHY

I am extremely grateful for the patient help of
Miss. P Bell and her staff at the County Record
Office, the staff at the County Local History Library
(now at Harper Street, Bedford), Dunstable Library,
Luton Library and Luton Museum, and to Mrs Rosemary
Harris for allowing me to use her research on the
Brandreth family.

Much of the medieval history of Houghton and also
background information concerning the nonconformist
movement is included in the publications of the
Bedfordshire Historical Record Society. There are
articles concerning the later history and in
particular the Quakers at Sewell in "The Bedfordshire
Magazine". Both of these publications are available
in the local reference libraries.

The 1851 and 1881 census are available on
microfiche at Luton Library and a complete set of
census is at the County Record Office.

By far the best book available about local history
is Miss J Godber's "Bedfordshire" (1969). The
prehistory of the area is covered in detail by
"Occupation Sites on a Chiltern Ridge", C L Matthews
(1976) and a more detailed history of Houghton is
available from the Book Castle, "The (Barracuda) Book
of Dunstable and Houghton Regis" by Vivienne and Lewis
Evans. All the references and rough notes used in the
preparation of both of these books is being deposited
with the Local History Librarian at Bedford, where
they will be available for consultation.

Vivienne Evans

# KEY TO ILLUSTRATIONS

Line drawings are all by Elizabeth Lowen except where indicated.

| | |
|---|---|
| FWP | F W Pratt |
| VML | Vauxhall Motors Ltd |
| OR | Omer Roucoux |
| LM | Luton Museum |
| CRO | County Record Office, Bedford |
| JB | J Beacon |
| JMB | J M Bailey |
| GN | Geoffrey Neal |
| TC | T Cumberland |
| AJ | Alan Johns, "The Crown" Inn |
| LF | L Fensome |
| HB | H Bandy |
| MD | Mrs M Day |
| DHHS | Dunstable Historic and Heritage Studies |
| BM | Mrs B Morton |
| GB | Guy Buckler |
| MG | M Giles |

# GLOSSARY

Advowson – The right of appointing a clergyman to a parish or other ecclesiastical benefice. An advowson is treated by English law as a right of property which can be transferred by gift or (until 1924) by sale. Nowadays the Diocesan Board usually presents candidates.

Chalice – The cup used to contain the wine at Communion.

Greater Tithes – The part of the tithes allocated at first to the monastery and later to the Lay Rector or Improprietor. The greater tithes represented about two thirds of the value of the whole tithes and consisted of the main crops – wheat, oats, etc.

Hide – A variable area of land, supposed to be an amount that would support one family. In Bedfordshire, about 120 acres.

Lay Rector – A layman receiving the rectorial tithes of a benefice. He has a legal duty to repair the chancel of the church.

Paten – The dish on which the bread is placed at Communion.

Patron – The owner of the right of advowson was known as the patron. He presented the candidate for a benefice to the bishop.

Piscina – (Latin-basin) A niche in a wall, usually on the south side of the altar, for the washing of the priests' hands, the chalice and the paten at Mass.

Pyx – A container for the bread used at Communion – especially for carrying Communion to the sick.

Rood – A representation of the Cross bearing the body of Christ, usually flanked by the Virgin & St John. The Rood Loft was a gallery for the Rood, sometimes big enough for the Gospel to be sung from it during Mass.

| | |
|---|---|
| Rood Screen | - A carved wooden or stone screen across the chancel. In medieval times it supported the Rood Loft. |
| Smaller Tithes | - This was the part of the tithes allocated to the Vicar. It represented about one third of the value of the total tithes but was made up of "minor produce" such as lambs, chickens, etc, and was difficult to collect. |
| Tithes | - A payment of one tenth part of all the produce of the land. As the parochial system developed the tithes of each parish were allotted to its own parson, the allocation becoming law in England in 900 A.D. The system was abolished beginning with the Tithe Act of 1936. |
| Trental | - A series of 30 Requiem Masses for the repose of the soul. Sometimes a Requiem Mass said 30 days after the death of the person concerned. |
| Vicar | - (latin vicarious - a substitute) The priest of a parish where the greater tithes went to someone else (a Lay Rector or Improprietor). In medieval times when churches were appropriated to monasteries, the monastery received the revenues and employed first one of their monks to perform the duties of Rector, later a secular priest, called a Vicar because he was the substitute for the religious house and received his payment "vicariously". |
| Vicarage | - A living where the greater tithes went to a Lay Rector. In modern times vicarage usually means the house where the incumbent lives. |

# INDEX

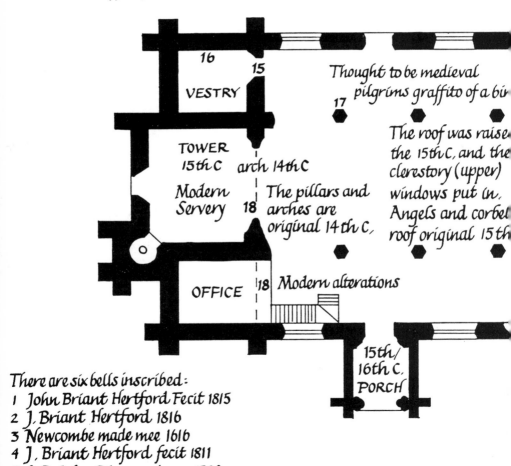

16 The Parish Registers
date from 1538
(Now in County Record
Office)

15 Board giving details
of Wm, Strange's
charity (1664)

16

15

VESTRY

Thought to be medieval
pilgrims graffito of a bir

17

TOWER
15th C    arch 14th C

Modern
Servery    18  The pillars and
arches are
original 14th C,

The roof was raise
the 15th C, and the
clerestory (upper)
windows put in.
Angels and corbel
roof original 15th

OFFICE    18  Modern alterations

15th/
16th C.
PORCH

There are six bells inscribed:
1 John Briant Hertford Fecit 1815
2 J, Briant Hertford 1816
3 Newcombe made mee 1616
4 J, Briant Hertford fecit 1811
5 O, B, John Dier made me 1580
6 Anthony Chandler made mee 1673
  (3rd and 5th recast 1899)
  The 5th bell is probably the earliest
  dated in the county

# N REGIS

Henry Brandreth (1610-1672) was Lord of the Manor of Houghton Regis, as were many Brandreths after him. He lived at the Manor House (not now in existence). His daughter Alice Milard built Houghton Hall, by the Green, and Brandreths lived there until 1913

Memorial window to Minna, daughter of Rev. Hugh Blaggmyth. Faces of children in central panel taken from photograph, early use of this medium in stained glass

8 Hatchment
Humphrey Brandreth
1807-1864

9 Memorial to Dame Alice Milard who built Houghton Hall in 1700

10 Replica of brass to Jn. Waleys

Chancel rebuilt 19c using many original 14th C materials

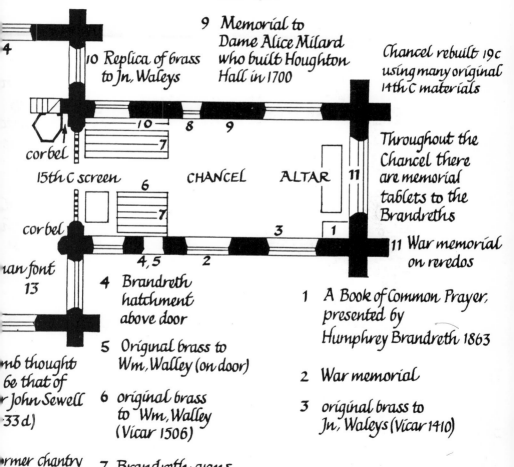

4

corbel

15th C screen

corbel

Norman font
13

Tomb thought to be that of Sir John Sewell (1433 d)

Former chantry chapel with 14th C. piscina

CHANCEL    ALTAR

Throughout the Chancel there are memorial tablets to the Brandreths

11 War memorial on reredos

4 Brandreth hatchment above door

5 Original brass to Wm. Walley (on door)

6 original brass to Wm. Walley (Vicar 1506)

7 Brandreth arms on pew-ends

1 A Book of Common Prayer, presented by Humphrey Brandreth 1863

2 War memorial

3 original brass to Jn. Waleys (Vicar 1410)